The Essen
Visual Communication

The Essential Guide to Visual Communication

Ryan McGeough

University of Northern Iowa

bedford/st.martin's
Macmillan Learning
Boston | New York

FOR BEDFORD/ST. MARTIN'S

Vice President, Editorial, Macmillan Learning Humanities: Edwin Hill
Senior Program Director for Communication: Erika Gutierrez
Marketing Manager: Amy Haines
Development Editor: Catherine Burgess
Assistant Editor: Kimberly Roberts
Senior Content Project Manager: Edward Dionne
Senior Workflow Project Supervisor: Joe Ford
Production Supervisor: Robin Besofsky
Senior Media Project Manager: Michelle Camisa
Senior Media Editor: Tom Kane
Editorial Services: Lumina Datamatics, Inc.
Composition: Lumina Datamatics, Inc.
Permissions Editor: Angela Boehler
Permissions Associate: Allison Ziebka
Photo Researcher: Brittani Morgan, Lumina Datamatics, Inc.
Director of Design, Content Management: Diana Blume
Text Design: Lumina Datamatics, Inc.
Cover Design: William Boardman
Printing and Binding: LSC Communications

Manufactured in the United States of America.

1   2   3   4   5   6   23   22   21   20   19

For information, write: Bedford/St. Martin's, 75 Arlington Street, Boston, MA 02116

ISBN 978-1-319-09417-1

Acknowledgments

Acknowledgments and copyrights appear on the same page as the text and art selections they cover; these acknowledgments and copyrights constitute an extension of the copyright page.

At the time of publication all Internet URLs published in this text were found to accurately link to their intended website. If you do find a broken link, please forward the information to kimberly.roberts@macmillan.com so that it can be corrected for the next printing.

To my mom and dad,
Coral and Denny McGeough,
who always encouraged me to see for myself.

PREFACE

The Essential Guide to Visual Communication is a versatile text for students who need a brief, topical introduction to key concepts in visual communication and visual rhetoric. It has been designed as a flexible option for use in a variety of communication courses, including introductory mass communication courses, classes that focus on improving students' media literacy skills, and any course where instructors want to give students a brief but thorough introduction to visual communication.

COVERAGE

The Essential Guide to Visual Communication helps students identify and understand core issues in visual communication and visual rhetoric quickly and effectively through an approach that combines a solid foundation in communication history and theory with a clear emphasis on developing skills in visual literacy. Topics include:

- Definition of visual communication and the processes by which we make meaning of visual messages (Chapter 1)
- The importance and necessity of studying visual communication in a world saturated with images (Chapter 1)
- Building blocks of visual communication: dots, lines, shapes, color, depth, motion (Chapter 2)
- Gestalt principles (Chapter 2)
- The development of communication technologies, from the printing press to new media, and the evolving impact of these technologies on politics and culture (Chapter 3)
- How images contribute to public memory, values, and identity, with a specific focus on iconic images, image events, monuments, and propaganda (Chapter 4)
- Types of signs embedded in visual communication (iconic, indexical, and symbolic) and the role of culture in shaping how we interpret and create meaning from visual communication (Chapter 5)

FEATURES

Throughout this text, you will find an assortment of features that will help you understand key concepts and assess your own learning. Images and figures provided in each chapter illustrate important ideas, theories, and moments in the history of visual communication. Additionally, checklists at the end of each chapter provide a quick means to ensure you understand what you've learned, and extended visual analyses apply key ideas using particular visual artifacts.

This book is available as a stand-alone text or packaged with *Media & Culture*, *Media Essentials, Media in Society*, and a number of other Bedford/St. Martin's communication titles. For more information about the Essential Guides, other books of interest, and custom options, visit macmillanlearning.com.

CONTENTS

Introduction to Visual Communication **1**

What do you see when you look at this April 2008 *Vogue* cover? What do you notice first? Your eyes could focus on the "87" on the left side of the cover or the words "Shape Issue" near the bottom, but chances are your eyes are first drawn to LeBron James and Gisele Bundchen, two recognizable pop culture figures who, presumably, appeal to *Vogue* readers. Take a moment to consider what you think is happening in this photo. What, exactly, do you see in the photo that informs what you think is happening?

Now, would it surprise you to learn that this magazine cover was very controversial?

At first glance, the elements of this *Vogue* cover seem fairly common. NBA star LeBron James appears to shout while standing with his left arm around smiling supermodel Gisele Bundchen as his right arm dribbles a basketball. The rest of the cover displays text including the title of the magazine and the contents within the issue. The magazine's title appears to be behind the two cover models,

whereas the rest of the text appears to be in front of them. Several of the elements in this image are similar to those we see on many other magazine covers. In isolation, this *Vogue* cover seems unremarkable.

But visual images never occur in isolation. A similar image appeared on a World War I recruiting poster for the U.S. Army from 1917 (left). This image portrays (1) a topless woman in a dress being carried in the left arm of a German "mad brute." The German appears as a gorilla walking onto the American shore with (2) his mouth agape and carrying in his right hand a club emblazoned with the word "Kultur." Playing on the racial and cultural prejudices of the time, the image represents Germans as barbaric animals and a threat to American women. Another similar image served as the promotional poster for the 1933 movie *King Kong* (right). Both the film and its promotional poster have long been accused of participating in damaging racial stereotypes: A dangerous, powerful, black animal is brought in chains from Africa to the United States, where he escapes and endangers a beautiful, innocent white woman. In the movie poster, the giant gorilla again stands with his mouth open, carrying a Caucasian woman in his left hand and batting at planes with his right.

Does knowing about these past images change how you interpret the *Vogue* cover? Does it give you a richer understanding of the image? It certainly makes the controversy surrounding the cover easier to understand: The cover became immensely controversial not because of the specific elements within the image, but because of its similarities and references to other images from the past. Many critics found it deeply problematic that one of America's most famous and financially successful African American men was on this cover in place of a gorilla. When combined with the United States's long history of characterizing African American men as a threat to white women, and the subsequent use of this threat as justification for violence against black men, it is not difficult to see why some found this cover image either distasteful or overtly racist.

Visual communication is the use of visual symbols to create and share meaning or to encourage action. Although the *Vogue* cover includes two incredibly famous people and generated substantial controversy, the story of this image is actually not so different from the story of most visual communication: The image competes against many other images for your attention, and multiple visual elements draw your eyes toward specific content that you must decode. Fully understanding the image requires you to recognize the cultural references connecting it to other pieces of visual communication. You may have walked right past this *Vogue* cover at almost any magazine stand or grocery store and barely noticed it among all the other mass-produced magazine covers. In order to fully make sense of the cover, you needed to pick it out from all the other mass-produced images surrounding it, analyze the particular content within the image, and understand the broader visual and cultural contexts with which it connects. This image of James and Bundchen is like all other images in that if you fail to attend to any one of these aspects of visual communication, you will have an incomplete understanding of the image. However, a viewer who knows *how* to look at an image will see more than just the elements on the page.

"THE MORE YOU KNOW, THE MORE YOU SEE."

These words, from author and philosopher Aldous Huxley, are at the heart of studying visual communication. Huxley, author of *Brave New World* (1932) and *After Many a Summer* (1939), went mostly blind for eighteen months from a corneal disease called *keratitis punctata* when he was sixteen years old (Lester, 2014). His vision improved as he got older, but he continued to have severely impaired sight, making him unable to pursue his plan of becoming a physician. The experience was formative for the young Huxley (Bedford, 2002). The loss of his sight altered how he thought about the world, and he even wrote about his struggles to re-teach himself to see in his 1942 book, *The Art of Seeing*. The book contains a variety of unusual (and largely disproven) exercises Huxley used to attempt to improve his eyesight, including relaxing the face and eyes and exposing them to increased sunlight. But its lasting contribution is Huxley's belief that seeing well is less about the natural ability of the eye and more about the well-trained mind. Huxley believed we could train ourselves to be more effective viewers of the world around us. Drawing on the thoughts of philosopher C. D. Broad, Huxley described seeing as consisting of three central processes: sensing, selecting, and perceiving.

SENSING

Sensing begins in the eye and is what we might consider the physiological act of seeing. In simple terms, sensing is the result of light bouncing off of objects and into the eye itself. Light enters the eye through the pupil: the small, black dot in the center of the eye. The pupil is ringed by a series of muscles known as the iris, which gives the eye its color. These muscles relax and contract in order to control how much light can pass through the pupil. The eye's lens then focuses the light onto the fovea—a tiny point on the rear of eye. The rear of the eye is known as the retina and is covered with over 100 million light-receptors called rods and cones. Rods are spread across the retina and allow us to see in low light and enable our low-detail, peripheral vision. Cones are concentrated in the fovea and allow us to perceive color and high levels of detail. When you walk through a dark room, seeing just enough detail to avoid obstacles, you rely on the data gained from rods. When you focus your eyes to read this sentence, you rely on data gained from cones. Both rods and cones respond to light by sending an electrical signal through the optical nerve to the brain. These signals travel to an area in the back of the brain known as the visual cortex. The visual cortex converts this series of electrical signals into what our brains understand as seeing, reconstructing millions of electrical impulses into the images we see (Tyley, 2015).

Huxley is correct that the physical process of sensing is only the beginning of seeing. But although sensing might initially seem like the simplest aspect of seeing, it still requires an amazing combination of physical processes in both the eye and the brain. Instantly and without conscious thought, your eye adjusts for the amount of light, millions of sensors in the eye respond to different wavelengths of light by producing electrical impulses, and your brain then reconstructs this torrent of electrical information into an impressively accurate picture of the world around you. This complex process occurs continuously, updating our brains multiple times per second, every waking moment of our lives.

SELECTING

In the process of sensing, the eye passes an incredible amount of information on to the brain. Take a moment to look around and consider just how many things your eyes sense. Notice all of the colors, lines, and shapes that make up all of the objects around you. You would find it impossible to process all of this information all of the time. Instead, you are constantly **selecting**: choosing particular visual stimuli to focus on. Huxley recognized this as an essential component of the process of seeing. Out of all of the visual information our eyes pass to our brains, our brains make the choice to select and focus on a limited subset. Even as you are reading this page, you can notice how the few words you are reading appear in sharp focus, while the words elsewhere on the page may appear blurry and unrecognizable. As we will discuss in the following chapters, some visual cues demand our attention, while others fade into the background. Selection allows the brain to ignore visual information you deem insignificant so that it can dedicate energy to aspects you deem important.

PERCEIVING

Once you have selected the visual information you wish to focus on, you begin what Huxley labeled perceiving. **Perceiving** is the mental process of making meaning out of visual stimuli. We might say that sensing is to hearing as selecting and perceiving are to listening. The former are automatic physiological processes that absorb information from the world around us. The latter are intentional acts in which we create meaning.

Huxley recognized that perceiving is intimately tied to memory. After selecting visual stimuli to focus on, we call on our existing memory and knowledge to quickly engage in the categorization and evaluation necessary to make sense of the stimuli. We answer questions such as: What colors and shapes do I see? Where have I seen them before? How should I respond to what I see? After we have interpreted them, the stimuli may be added to our memory where they will become part of how we interpret future stimuli.

Imagine you are walking across campus. Out of the wealth of visual stimuli you sense, you quickly select a dog running toward you. If the dog looked like a dog that had bitten you in the past, this would likely lead you to perceive the oncoming dog as a threat and perhaps compel you to try to escape. But if the dog resembled a childhood pet or your neighbor's dog, you might instead call out to it or reach out your hand. Either one of these perceptions would be logical based upon your past experiences. If, upon reaching you, the dog immediately rolled over and begged you to pet it, this memory would likely impact how you perceive a dog you see running free in the future.

The point here is twofold. First, how we perceive what we see is strongly affected by past perceptions. Some aspects of seeing, such as the eye being drawn to motion, are relatively universal (we will discuss those aspects in Chapter 2), but most are culturally and individually specific (we will discuss those aspects in Chapters 4 and 5). Second, perception is an ongoing process. Your latest experience with the oncoming dog will influence your next experience. When we perceive stimuli, we not only draw on past memories, we create new memories.

WHY STUDY VISUAL COMMUNICATION?

Visual images surround us. Every day we are inundated with images from computer screens, tablets, cell phones, televisions, magazine covers, movie screens, bumper stickers, t-shirts, yard signs, architecture, hats, business signs, tattoos, sneakers, and many more. Because of their ubiquity, we pass many of them without paying much attention (think of the dozens of images you pass every time you walk past a news-stand or magazine rack). Some we stop and consider carefully (as you might look closely at a book cover that interests you or a tattoo on someone sitting next to you in class), while many others we respond to habitually, but without much thought (as you might stop for a red light or wait for the white walking symbol before crossing the street at a crosswalk). The combined power of instinctive responses, individual experiences, and cultural norms surrounding visual cues makes visual images a central part of how we navigate the world.

Technological advances have made exposure to visual images much more common. We'll take a look at some of the most important of these technologies—ranging from the printing press to the Internet—in greater detail in Chapter 3. Technologies that you may rely on daily, such as smart phones or laptops, have made visual communication more widespread than ever before. At no point in history have as many people had access to as many images or the ability to visually communicate to so many other people as they do now. As more people gain access to these technologies and media such as Facebook or Snapchat make the Internet even more image-based, it is becoming more important than ever to know how to be a savvy and effective visual communicator.

Visual communication is particularly fascinating because it encompasses many aspects of how we interact with one another and make sense of the world; most of the information we gather about the world around us and how to respond to it comes from visual sources. Visual communication plays a vital role in how we answer a huge variety of questions ranging from "Who should we date?" to "What should we buy?" to "Who should be allowed to enter our country?" Because of the breadth and importance of visual communication, it is studied inside and outside of academia by researchers in a variety of fields including communication studies, art, English, political science, philosophy, marketing, business, linguistics, and psychology. Studying visual communication means becoming attuned to the choices involved in creating visual elements, from the seemingly simple, such as placing a dot on a page, to the complex, such as deciding how a war memorial should visually represent the sacrifice of fallen soldiers (as we will discuss in Chapter 4).

This ability to skillfully make sense of visual communication is known as **visual literacy.** Anne Bamford (2003) describes visual literacy as "developing the set of skills needed to be able to interpret the content of visual images, [to] examine social impact[s] of those images and to discuss purpose, audience and ownership. . . [and] to be aware of the manipulative uses and ideological implications of images" (p. 1). Our world is awash in visual communication: Corporations spend billions of dollars per year on visual advertising in order to get your money, politicians create advertisements in order to get your vote, and employers make hiring decisions based on how you visually present yourself on your résumé or Facebook. In our world, few skills are as valuable as visual literacy.

Just as we define literacy as the ability to read and write, visual literacy requires being able to both interpret and create visual symbols. Although in this text we will focus primarily on becoming more skilled *interpreters* of visual images, having the knowledge and skills to do so will also make you more effective at *creating* them. As with reading words, we make sense of images using particular rules and conventions; knowing these rules and conventions will help you anticipate how others will interpret and respond to the various types of visual messages you create. Further, knowing how our eyes and brains naturally tend to process images, as well as understanding the technological, rhetorical, and cultural aspects of an image, will allow you to take a more active and informed role in how you respond to images you see. This knowledge will help you more competently engage in visual communication.

Developing visual literacy is possible because our interpretations of visual images are connected. **Intertextuality** refers to the way that every text and image draws on and connects to past texts and images. Roland Barthes (1977) argues that new creations can never be original, but rather that each new text is "a multidimensional space in which a variety of writings, none of them original, blend and clash" (p. 146). These connections between texts occur in part as artists borrow from and are influenced by other artists. When you create an image, you cannot help but be influenced by past images that you have seen. Whether you are creating an advertisement, photograph, or website, your choices will be at least partially informed by past advertisements, photographs, or websites you have seen. But the connections between texts go beyond the image creator's past influences. As viewers, we can never perceive an image objectively; we always bring our own perspective to the image, as well as the particular conventions we have been taught about how to "read" an image. These learned conventions condition us to automatically—and often uncritically—make sense of the images we see.

What are these conventions? We will discuss them in the ensuing chapters, in which we consider how our eyes and brains naturally respond to specific visual elements, how visual communication evolved, how visual rhetoric and persuasion function, and how images operate within our increasingly visual cultures. Through this we will recognize that just because we have been conditioned into particular habits of looking does not mean that *seeing* needs to remain a passive process. As Aldous Huxley recognized, by studying visual communication, we can learn to see *more*. In so doing, we can learn to become more critical consumers and skillful producers of images.

CHECKLIST: UNDERSTANDING VISUAL COMMUNICATION

Select an image that you find interesting. Ask yourself the following questions:

✓ Why did you choose this image?

✓ Which elements of the image seem most interesting or important? Why?

✓ What do you think the creator of the image was trying to communicate? How do you know?

✓ How does this image relate to other images you have seen? How is it similar? How is it different?

✓ What are the broader visual and cultural contexts this image connects to?

2 *Visual Composition and Design*

When humans learn to communicate verbally, we first learn specific words and sounds, and eventually build the ability to give a speech or easily carry on a complex conversation. Visual communication functions similarly. Even the most beautiful works of art or most effective propaganda posters are built from basic building blocks. These may be things that you have seen thousands of times and have paid little attention to (or never noticed), but they can have profound effects on how we interpret images. Again, the more you *know*, the more you *see*.

In this chapter, we'll discuss some of the basic design elements that comprise visual images. These basic building blocks include composition; visual forms of dots, lines, and shapes; the Gestalt principles; and color, depth, and motion. Understanding these concepts will provide you with the tools to recognize how visual images are constructed and how our eyes and brains interpret them.

THE BUILDING BLOCKS OF VISUAL COMMUNICATION

From the complicated physiological process of seeing to the subtle ways images can foster desire or create community, visual communication is an incredibly complex process. Yet, visual images are ultimately comprised of a few, simple components. We begin with composition.

COMPOSITION

If you have ever begun to take a photograph, only to pause and move the camera in order to improve the photo, you have made an intentional choice about composition. **Composition** is the way in which the visual elements of an image are situated within a frame. Composition is important because how and where the contents of an image are placed within a frame can change how viewers interpret an image. For example, when we look at an image in which two people appear in the middle of the frame, we tend to perceive them as comfortable. You may notice in talk shows that the interviewer and guest are almost humorously close together. Placing them both in the center of the frame puts the audience at ease by creating the visual impression of a pleasant conversation (Fabos, 2013). On the other hand, placing people near the edges of the frame creates the impression of tension between them. This effect is the result of **frame magnetism**, the visual illusion created when the nearer an object is to the edge of a rectangular frame, the stronger it seems that the object is being pulled toward that edge. This is why placing two people near the edges of an image creates a feeling of tension—they appear to be pulled in opposite directions by the frame on either side.

Although frame magnetism may seem like something to avoid, it can also be used to create more dynamic, interesting images. Frame magnetism is the visual effect at work behind the **Rule of Thirds**. The Rule of Thirds is a famous photographic principle that suggests that by breaking an image into thirds both vertically and horizontally, and placing visually important parts of the image at the intersection of these thirds, we can create a more interesting image.

We can see frame magnetism and the Rule of Thirds in Figure 2.1. Placing the Eiffel Tower near the left-grid intersections pulls it toward the left frame and creates an imbalance in the image. This lack of balance makes the image more visually interesting than if the tower were centered in the frame. Meanwhile, the two lower grid intersections fall on the horizon line created by the trees and buildings. This creates a feeling of openness, as the sky occupies the upper two-thirds of the image, while the water and bridge are pulled toward the bottom of the frame.

DOTS

A small, round point in space, the **dot** is the most basic and fundamental building block of visual communication. Creating a dot is as simple as touching a pen to a piece of paper, yet dots can have powerful effects on how we view an image.

Courtesy of Ryan McGeough

Figure 2.1

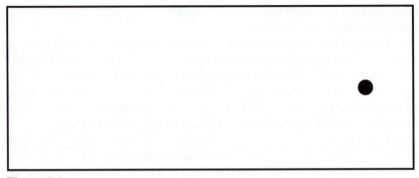

Figure 2.2

Place a dot anywhere on an image—with or without other shapes—and the eye is naturally drawn to it (Figure 2.2).

Place a series of dots in a row, and we naturally connect them to form a line (Figure 2.3). The closer the dots are to one another, the more strongly our minds perceive the line.

The famous pointillist painter Georges Seurat discovered that by covering his canvas in thousands of tiny dots, he could create intricate images of people and landscapes. In this same way, dots make up the images that you see on your computer, phone, and television screens, but we see them constantly without even noticing them—as pixels. The difference between older, grainier screens and newer, high-resolution screens is simply the number and size of the pixels.

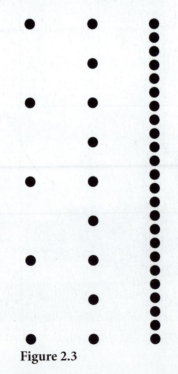

Figure 2.3

If you look incredibly closely at a Seurat painting, or your computer screen, you will notice the tiny dots making up the image. Most of the time, however, your brain simply combines them into images without any conscious effort.

LINES AND SHAPES

When a series of dots are placed together without any space between them, they create **lines**. We tend to seek out lines because they help us identify shapes and distinguish between forms within an image. Lines also impact our emotional responses to images. Horizontal lines tend to evoke a sense of stability within the image, carrying our eyes across the page. Vertical lines tend to evoke a sense of energy. They also create breaks in the layout of an image; multiple vertical lines may potentially encourage us to look at one image as a series of images. In a graphic novel, for example, the animated panels are separated by short vertical spaces. These vertical lines (known as gutters) help viewers see each panel as a distinct moment within a sequence. A vertical line placed in the center of an image may create a sense of tension or balance between the contents of either side of the image. Look at Figure 2.4. The vertical line in this promotional poster for the final movie in the Harry Potter series divides the image in a way that

Figure 2.4

heightens the sense of tension. In this poster, the protagonist of the series, Harry Potter, and the antagonist, the evil wizard Voldemort, stare from either side of the image. The implied horizontal line connecting their eyes (1) draws the viewer's gaze to the space between them. The vertical line of the wand (2) separates the page down the center, suggesting not just a tension between the two, but also a balance. Fans of the series would recognize this as a visual representation of the plot of the series: a clash between the two in which neither was able to completely defeat the other. Fans would also know that the wand dividing them was a particularly powerful wand that Voldemort had found at the end of the previous movie. Thus, the vertical line not only represents the tension and balance between the two characters, but also the promise that—in the final film—this balance would be broken. The implications of these visual cues are made explicit in the poster's caption (3): "IT ALL ENDS."

Diagonal lines are the most visually powerful, immediately grabbing the viewer's attention and causing the eye to follow the path of the line. Theorists have speculated that diagonal lines are particularly powerful because they indicate flux and a lack of equilibrium. As you can see in Figure 2.5, even a common shape such as (1) the outline of a car—when placed at a diagonal—invites a closer look. When combined with shifting, diagonal lines (2), the outline of the car appears unbalanced, in transition, or potentially as falling. The possible

Zoart Studio/Shutterstock

Figure 2.5

exception to this tendency is the 45-degree diagonal line, which is less visually demanding than other diagonals because it divides the space in half and thus creates an even balance on either side.

Lines can also combine to form the outline of shapes, objects whose contours we recognize as belonging together and thus distinct from other elements of an image. Basic shapes include circles, squares, and triangles; more complex shapes are generally formed by combinations and variations of these three (Dondis, 1973).

Shapes are visually powerful because they are a visual pattern that we recognize. For example, the *Vogue* cover with LeBron James and Giselle Bundchen from the previous chapter includes a circle-shaped object in the lower left corner of the cover. For most viewers, the brain automatically recognizes the circle as a basketball, and thus an object distinct from the other elements of the magazine cover. We can often recognize even very simple combinations of lines as representing more complex shapes. In the sign in Figure 2.5, we see a relatively simple combination of lines and recognize the shape as a car.

GESTALT

Gestalt psychology emerged from the Berlin School of Experimental Psychology in the early 20th century, and its principles extend to how we study visual communication. Gestalt psychology begins with the premise that human perceptions are the result of complex combinations of stimuli. How the brain processes these combinations leads to new perceptions that transcend the individual stimuli themselves. As Gestalt psychologist Kurt Koffka famously stated, "The whole is other than the sum of its parts" (Wong, 2010). What does this mean in the context of visual communication? When we look at an image, **Gestalt** refers to how we perceive a whole that cannot be described simply by describing the visual elements that make up the image. The psychologist Max Wertheimer (1938) observed a number of principles that help us understand how Gestalt works in visual communication, particularly in terms of the visual associations our brain makes between objects. These principles include the principle of similarity, the principle of proximity, the principle of continuation, the principle of closure, and the principle of common fate.

Similarity
The Gestalt principle of similarity states that we tend to mentally group things that are similar in appearance. Similarities—including size, shape, color, and location—lead us to perceive objects as members of a set. For example, take a look at Figure 2.6. The principle of similarity is why you likely identified the filled-in black squares as a set, the unfilled white squares as a different set, and the circles in the middle as a separate set. This principle is particularly powerful when one or two objects are dissimilar from the rest.

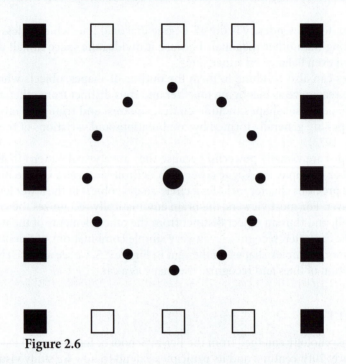

Figure 2.6

Proximity

The Gestalt principle of proximity, a subset of the principle of similarity, states that we tend to recognize things that are close to one another as members of a group. Their similarity is in their location within an image. Look at Figure 2.7: Here, your mind likely perceives the eight pentagons as distinct and individual shapes. Now, look at Figure 2.8: Here, the same eight shapes appear as members

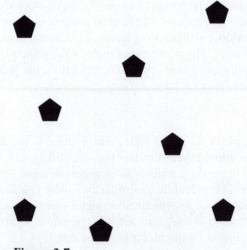

Figure 2.7

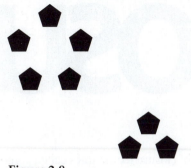

Figure 2.8

of two distinct groups. The principle of proximity constantly affects how we make sense of the world around us. The next time you walk on campus, pay attention to how you perceive the people around you. You are likely to find that you assume people standing near one another to be intentionally together, even if they are not interacting in any other way. The closer things are to one another, the stronger our minds view them as a group.

Continuation

The Gestalt principle of continuation describes our tendency to continue to follow a line or curve from one object to the next and perceive all of the connected elements to be part of the same line. Because our brains try to continue a line in the direction it is moving, we follow the path of a line or curve even if it temporarily disappears from our vision, and we assume that it continues even when we cannot see it. Look at Figure 2.9. What do you see at first glance? Now, look more closely. What, exactly, do you see? What we really see in this image are the letters GESTALT, with a series of short, horizontal line segments running between each of the letters. The principle of continuation accounts for what we actually perceive: one long arrow running behind all of the letters. We cannot see if the horizontal line segments connect, but because they all run along the same perceived line, we expect them to be connected. We mentally separate them as part of an arrow separate from the letters.

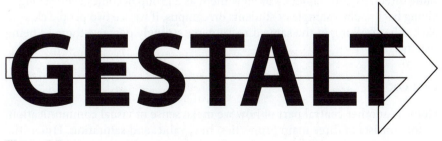

Figure 2.9

CLOSURE

Figure 2.10

Closure
The Gestalt principle of closure (sometimes called completion) is related to the principle of continuation, in that the brain naturally fills in a missing line in order to complete a shape (Kanizsa, 1979). When you look at Figure 2.10, you see the R in the negative space without having to think about it. Part of this is due to your eye naturally continuing the curve of the top of the letter, but part is also due to your familiarity with the shape of the letter R. The more familiar you are with a shape, the more naturally and quickly your mind will engage in closure if part of the shape is missing.

The importance of familiarity in the principle of closure highlights the importance of audience analysis when creating visual images. Any audience member is likely to continue the curve at the top of the letter. However, an audience member whose native language includes the letter R is much more likely to automatically recognize it as a familiar shape. Audience members who are less familiar with the letter R (for example, an audience member whose first language is Arabic or Mandarin) might not be as familiar with the shape of the letter, and might be less likely to engage in closure as the creator of the image intended.

Common Fate
The Gestalt principle of common fate describes our tendency to perceive objects that are—or appear to be—moving in the same direction as part of a group. Look at Figure 2.11. All of the scissors are centered in the middle of the page, yet our natural tendency is to perceive them as two distinct groups. We see one group of scissors cutting to the left, and another group cutting to the right. The principle of common fate can work powerfully in tandem with the principle of proximity. If several objects are near one another and appear to be moving in the same direction, our tendency to view them as a group becomes even stronger. Going back to the example of students on campus, if we see two people close to each other walking in the same direction, we strongly perceive them as being together.

COLOR

Color is another central part of how we make sense of visual communication. Color consists of three main properties: hue, value, and saturation. **Hue** is the

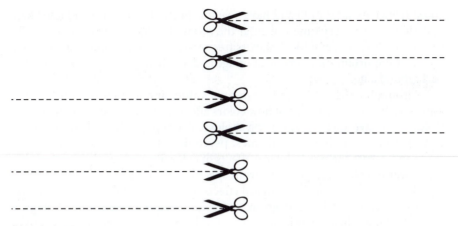

Figure 2.11

term for a particular color; blue, yellow, and red are names we use for various hues. Hues form when light reflects off of objects. White light, such as sunlight or the light from most light bulbs, actually contains many hues within it. If you have ever seen a prism or a rainbow, you have seen white light separated into its many constitutive hues. Different objects in the world reflect slightly different wavelengths of this light, which is why they appear to be different hues. Humans can only see a tiny segment of these wavelengths, while other shorter wavelengths of light (such as UV light) or longer wavelengths of light (such as microwaves) remain invisible to us. The narrow part of the spectrum that we can see provides the multitude of colors around us.

Value refers to the darkness or lightness of a particular hue. Any given hue might be perceived as many different colors depending upon how dark or light its value. For example, both a pale blue and deep navy blue exist as part of the hue we call "blue," but they might appear as substantially different colors to us: The former may appear close to white and the latter may appear nearly black. Both are blue, but they differ in value. Value also affects our brain's perception of depth, as darker versions of a color seem closer to the foreground, while lighter values of the same color seem to recede into the background.

Saturation is the purity and intensity of a color. Whereas the value of a color occurs on a continuum from near-white to near-black, saturation occurs on a continuum from the specific hue to gray. For example, if you drive through a construction area on a highway, you may see yellow warning signs and orange traffic cones. The colors of these objects are highly saturated. The intensity of the colors causes the signs and the cones to leap out from their surroundings when we pass them. The capacity of highly saturated colors to pop out from their surroundings makes them an excellent visual choice for street signs, school buses, and any other visual design element intended to grab the eye. If you wanted to paint a room in your apartment yellow, however, you probably would not want a color with the same intense saturation. By mixing gray with the yellow, you could reduce its saturation and have a yellow that is less intense and less likely to grab your eye every time you enter the room. Because our eyes are naturally drawn to saturation, graphic designers frequently use highly saturated colors for the most important elements of an image and set them against lower saturated background colors.

Although color is formed from hue, value, and saturation, these three aspects only account for part of how colors affect the way we perceive the world. Colors also have a wide array of psychological and physiological effects on us. In fact, a huge number of academics, psychologists, and market researchers study and debate the psychological effects of color. Researchers have found that the power of color emerges both from specific cultural associations as well as broader, more universal physiological effects. Advertisers and marketing experts believe that colors such as red, green, and blue can have important psychological effects that may change our behaviors and influence our purchasing decisions.

Red is the color most studied by researchers. It is frequently associated with blood, passion, sex, and aggression. A word for red appears in virtually every language, and it is almost universally the first color to appear in each language (Loreto, Mukherjee, and Tria, 2012). Red may be the color most likely to transcend particular cultural associations because of its relationship to blood. For example, red has long been associated with both sexual arousal and anger in many different cultures, which is likely due to the flushing of the face during feelings of desire or anger. These ties to reproduction and danger make an awareness of red particularly important from an evolutionary perspective. Researchers have found that women wearing red clothing are perceived as more attractive and sexually available than women dressed in other hues (Elliot and Niesta, 2008). Women wearing red in their online dating profiles were more likely to get responses than those in other colors (Guéguen and Jacob, 2013). This effect has even been found when women stand near red objects or in front of a red background.

The color red may also prompt us to eat more food. Researchers have offered several possible explanations for this phenomenon, but marketing experts consistently use it to entice us to buy more of their company's food. Consider your favorite fast-food restaurant. Does it have red in its logo? If you chose McDonalds, Wendy's, Burger King, Hardees, Carl's Jr., Pizza Hut, Chick-fil-A, Dairy Queen, Popeye's, or Jack in the Box, the answer is yes (Newbold, 2013). When designing a logo for a new fast-food restaurant, designers obviously have an incentive to create a logo that sticks out from the rest. But even so, newer competitors in the fast-food market, such as Five Guys or Smash Burger, still choose red because they believe in its power to influence our behavior.

Green is frequently associated with nature, life, and the environment. When a company tries to reduce their environmental impact, we talk about how they are "going green." In the United States, green is also associated with wealth and money. Green has largely positive associations and is often used in locations such as luxury spas to create visual environments that feel calm and relaxing.

Blue is commonly associated with security, honesty, and trustworthiness (Arntson, 2012). This may be why it is commonly found in the logos of banks, insurance companies, and other financial institutions—places in which we want to feel we can trust how our money is kept and used. Like green, blue also has a calming effect that relaxes and slows us down. You can find blue commonly used in the logos or background colors of Internet sites such as Facebook, Twitter, Tumblr, LinkedIn, or Pandora, which make money by keeping users continuously viewing their pages. It is unsurprising that they would choose colors intended to calm their viewers.

DEPTH

One of the most useful aspects of vision is the ability to perceive depth. **Depth** is how close or far away an object is, particularly in relation to other objects. Depth perception allows us to do things as evolutionarily useful as recognizing that something is approaching or as socially useful as giving someone a high five without completely missing their hand. Our brains dedicate substantial resources to recognizing and calculating depth, and they do so unconsciously. Most of our perception of depth occurs in the three-dimensional space of the world around us, although we can also recognize depth (or at least the illusion of depth) in two-dimensional images.

How do we recognize depth in the world around us? As you might have guessed, part of our ability to do so comes from having two eyes, a feature called *stereoscopic vision*. If you were to close one eye and look around the room, and then close the other eye and look again, you would probably not notice much of a difference. Yet small differences do exist. Take a pen and put it midway between your eye and this book. Keeping your eyes focused on the book, close one eye. Then open that eye and close the other. The pen appears to move because of the slightly different perspective of each eye. You normally do not notice this shift because your brain automatically synthesizes the information it collects from both eyes, but that shift demonstrates an important part of how our eyes and brain perceive depth. Now repeat the pen exercise, but position the pen just an inch or two in front of your face. This time it will appear to move substantially across your field of vision. The closer objects are to us, the greater the difference between what each of our eyes sees. The brain accounts for the differences between what each eye senses and uses these differences to calculate depth. Of course, stereoscopic vision accounts for only one way in which we are able to perceive depth. Even when looking at two-dimensional images, our brains recognize visual cues such as size and perspective that also assist us in the three-dimensional world. These cues help us perceive depth even in images printed on a flat surface.

Size and perspective, perhaps the most powerful depth cues, make objects situated closer to the viewer appear larger, and those further away appear smaller. Or rather, objects situated closer to the viewer occupy more of our visual field and objects situated further away occupy less of our visual field. Yet, we do not necessarily perceive them to actually be larger or smaller. Instead, we perceive them to be nearer or further away from us. This is particularly true—and almost automatically done by our brains—if we believe that we know the size of the objects. For example, it's popular for vacationers to take photos of themselves "holding up" the Leaning Tower of Pisa or putting their finger "on top of" the Eiffel Tower. In these types of photos, we almost automatically recognize that the person is simply closer to us than the structure. Though typically useful, the brain's natural judgments about depth are not always accurate. Take a moment to go to YouTube and watch, "Criss Angel BeLIEve: Criss Angel Magic Revealed." Notice how what initially appears to be a normal-sized chair is actually revealed to be tiny, while the seemingly normal-sized wine glass is actually much larger than the chair. Illusionist Criss Angel creates these illusions by placing the objects at different depths from the viewer's perspective, and letting our brains do the rest.

MOTION

Out of all of the visual cues described in this chapter, **motion**, the illusion of movement in an image, most powerfully demands our attention. When a dot is set against a background of various colors, differing lights, and intersecting lines, our eyes will focus on and track it as it seems to move about the image. This focus on motion likely has an evolutionary origin: Quickly picking out an animal approaching in the distance from all other visual stimuli would have given our ancestors time to prepare for fight or flight. While approaching lions are no longer a major concern for most of us, our eyes are still more alert to motion than any other visual cue.

In the context of visual communication, motion is an *illusion* because, no matter how strongly our brain senses motion, most of the visual images we consume do not actually move. Instead, they provide particular visual cues that align with how we see motion in the physical world. These cues take the form of implied motion and apparent motion.

Implied motion is the illusion of movement within a single image, such as a photograph or illustration within a comic book. Imagine or search online for a photograph of a basketball player jumping to shoot a basketball. The image may capture the player in the air with the ball inches above his hands, but what do we see, exactly? We see an athlete and ball appearing to float in midair. Our brain recognizes, however, that the photograph actually captures a more complex movement. Look at Figure 2.12. What do you think is happening here? The superhero in the illustration appears to be punching a villain. But how can we tell that from a still image? The lines coming from the hero's fist (1) and arm, as well as the word "POW!" (2), make clear that he is in the act of throwing a punch. The diagonal lines of both the hero and villain help us perceive that they are moving. This illustration typifies how many comics use implied motion to help us imagine motion without motion picture technology.

drante/Getty Images

Figure 2.12

One of the greatest advances in visual communication was the motion picture (discussed in the following chapter), whose technology allowed for the creation of movies and television. The "motion" involved in motion pictures is **apparent motion**, the illusion of motion we perceive when multiple still images are displayed in rapid sequence. Consider the massive reels of film used in movie theatres: Each reel may contain over 10,000 still images. When those images are shown in rapid succession—typically between 16 and 24 per second—our brains perceive fluid movement rather than a series of pictures. This same effect governs our perception of all animations, ranging from simple cartoon flip-books to intricately drawn Disney films. To see apparent motion in action, draw a simple cartoon figure multiple times on sequential pages of a small notepad, making sure the figure progresses through slightly different positions. Then using your thumb to quickly flip through those pages, you can create the illusion of apparent motion.

Apparent motion is possible because of a phenomenon known as the *persistence of vision*. Early studies on persistence of vision suggested that each of the rapidly sequenced images makes an impression on the retina, only to have the next image appear before the previous one has time to fade. In other words, persistence of vision was believed to be the result of images continuously piling up and leaving traces on the retina, which creates an illusion in which they blend together. More recent scholarship challenges this explanation: Researchers now believe that persistence of vision occurs not on the retina, but in the brain (Anderson and Anderson, 1993). Because the brain requires roughly one-tenth of a second to process an image, when sequenced images are displayed more quickly than this, our brain—not our eyes—perceives this as motion.

CHECKLIST: UNDERSTANDING BASIC DESIGN PRINCIPLES

✓ Where are the key elements placed within the frame of the image?

✓ How does the placement of these elements affect how you perceive them?

✓ Are vertical, horizontal, or diagonal lines prominent in the image?

✓ Which elements do you perceive as belonging together? Why?

✓ Which colors are most prominent in the image? How do they affect your perception?

✓ Do you perceive some visual elements as closer or further than one another? Why?

✓ Do any elements in the image appear be moving? How can you tell?

ANALYZING VISUAL COMMUNICATION

Look at this painting by the famous graffiti artist Banksy. To see this image in greater detail or in color, search online for "Banksy, Birds on a Wire." Applying the concepts and principles from this chapter, what do you see now that you would not have seen before?

1. **Proximity:** When you first looked at this image, did you automatically see the birds on the left as a group? Why? Notice the small spacing between the birds on the left and larger space between them and the single bird on the right. The rule of proximity states that we tend to view objects that are placed closely together as a group. This is especially true when most of them are facing in the same direction (which also creates a sense of common fate).

2. **Closure:** At first glance, you probably perceive the line/crack upon which the birds are standing as running continuously across the image. Look more closely, and you will notice several places in which the line is actually interrupted. As discussed earlier, the human brain resists unpredictable changes in a line and actually attempts to continue the line, even where it is not present.

3. **Color:** In this image, color provides another clear distinction between the group on the left and the single bird on the right. Although most of the painting is on the left of the image, if you view a full color version of the image, your eyes are likely to come to rest on the smaller bird because its bright green contrasts sharply with the muted greys constituting the rest of the image.

4. **Depth/perspective:** We believe the bird on the right is smaller because we perceive it to be on the same depth plane (the wire) as the other birds. Without the wire, we might perceive the bird to simply be further away.

3 *Visual Communication and Technology*

The history of visual communication is a history of technological innovation. To understand how visual communication has changed over time, we must understand how new technologies let people share and consume visual content in new ways.

The famous media theorist Marshall McLuhan claimed that a medium is simply an extension of our senses. Visual media allow us to see things that we could not have seen before. Viewers of nightly news programs are able to see events occurring all over the world—sometimes just moments after they happen. For most of human history, a conversation required two people to be physically close to one another; today, numerous technologies allow us to see and hear one another in real time across thousands of miles. Technologies that allow us to see in new ways enable us to think, communicate, and act in new ways as well. This chapter considers a handful of particularly important technologies that have vastly extended our ability to see.

VISUAL COMMUNICATION TECHNOLOGIES

Four technologies have been particularly powerful in transforming how we communicate with one another: the printing press, the photograph, the motion picture, and the Internet. Although we may not always think of them this way, each of these technologies changed the world by changing what people were able to see. Each expanded access by allowing a greater number of people to either create or consume visual information. These different technologies also enabled visual information to circulate in different ways; in so doing, they encouraged users to have particular relationships with the visual content—and with each other.

Visual communication technologies have powerful effects on how we interact with one another and what social organizations we form. Technologies change our interactions and social organizations not by forcing us to think, communicate, or organize in one specific way or another, but by making some interactions easier and others more difficult (Innis, 1951). By making one type of communication easier, a technology makes us more likely to engage in that type of communication (and thus less likely to engage in other types of communication). For example, text messaging technologies have made it incredibly easy to exchange short written messages. As a result, you may be less likely to call someone on the phone because you can exchange text messages instead.

The same logic applies to social and political organizations. As visual communication technologies have evolved, new technologies have made it possible to create new types of social organizations. For example, the Internet has made it easier for fans of an artist or supporters of a little-known political candidate to create groups to promote them. When technologies enable us to communicate and organize in new ways—often through the circulation of visual content— they frequently disrupt our existing patterns of communication. This chapter explores the origins of four such disruptive visual technologies, as well as how each has changed our social or political interactions with one another.

THE PRINTING PRESS

Around the year 1440, Johannes Gutenberg completed development of one of the most important inventions in history: the **printing press**. Gutenberg's printing press was the result of years of experimenting with existing technologies and researching new ones. Like all visual communication technologies, it drew heavily on media that preceded it. The printing press combined several technologies: the Roman screw press, invented in the 1st century C.E. and used for pressing grapes to make wine; movable type, first invented for a Chinese version of the printing press in the 11th century; metal type blocks created in Korea in 1234; the codex, a collection of pages bound on one side—like this book—that replaced the scroll throughout the Roman empire during the 1st through 5th centuries C.E.; oil-based inks; and a variety of types of pages including parchment and paper, which became economical because of hydro-powered paper mills of the 13th century (Febvre and Martin, 1976). Gutenberg adapted these technologies, making metal type from various alloys and ink from various oils, until he found a combination that allowed him to reproduce pages much more quickly and economically than had ever been possible before. The printing press allowed the creation and circulation of visual content—including words and images—at a speed previously unimaginable.

It would be difficult to overstate the impact of the printing press on European civilization. Gutenberg developed his printing press as a business venture to allow the fast and relatively inexpensive reproduction of Bibles. Prior to the printing press, Bibles were primarily produced by monks who had to copy them by hand—a tedious process that made copies of the Bible rare, expensive, and available almost exclusively in Latin. The printing press allowed the mass production of Bibles in different languages. Suddenly, middle class Europeans could afford Bibles in their native languages and read scripture for themselves. It is no coincidence that the spread of the printing press was followed by the Protestant Reformation, in which several groups broke away from the Catholic Church and formed new denominations.

The newfound ability to disseminate information across long distances contributed to many other social changes. When books had been prohibitively expensive, the average person had little incentive to learn to read. However, as books became more easily attainable, literacy rates began steadily increasing and private libraries became more common. A greater concentration of books and libraries made major cities into increasingly potent hubs of intellectual exchange. By allowing scholars, authors, and artists to engage with one another's ideas more easily, the printing press accelerated the Renaissance. In these ways, the printing press helped foster a rapid increase in scientific and technological advances.

Similarly, the printing press helped set the stage for the Industrial Revolution. As the newly literate middle class began investing in newly developed technologies, an ever-growing number of factories sprang up in most cities, flooding the market with new goods. As manufacturers recognized that they needed to distinguish their products and convince potential customers to buy them, another social practice became common: advertising. Newspapers—yet another technology made possible by the printing press—began selling space to manufacturers to market and sell products.

Early advertisements were primarily text-based, but by the mid-1800s, advertisers began pioneering a number of advertising techniques that remain common today. They developed slogans for companies and paired the text with images designed to evoke particular emotions or responses from viewers. For example, in 1911, the Woodbury Soap Company adopted the slogan "skin you love to touch" along with a depiction of a man caressing a woman—thus pioneering the now ubiquitous practice of using sex to market products.

PHOTOGRAPHY

After spending the 1820s developing a primitive photographic technique that relied on using sunlight to bake an image in asphalt, Joseph Nicéphore Niépce partnered with Louis Daguerre to create the first camera capable of taking crisp images with relatively little exposure time. They developed a metallic compound that, when placed in a camera obscura and exposed to light, would take on the imprint of an image. Unlike Niépce's earlier techniques, which took up to eight hours to develop, the new technology, called the **daguerreotype**, could produce images in under fifteen minutes. Within a few years, more advanced daguerreotypes could capture an image in under a minute. In 1839, France purchased the rights to the technology and released the details of the daguerreotype manufacturing and developing processes freely as a gift to the world. The daguerreotype democratized the image by making individual and family portraits affordable and accessible to those who could not afford to commission a painting of themselves. As the daguerreotype and related techniques quickly spread throughout Europe and into North America, they were given a name that might seem more familiar: photography.

The appeal of photography was broad and powerful. Several other technological advances—most notably film—made photography faster and readily reproducible. But as with most new technologies, the major barrier to photography becoming truly widespread was convenience. That convenience barrier was shattered in 1888 by George Eastman, who developed Kodak cameras—relatively inexpensive devices that came preloaded with rolls of film. After using all of the film in the camera, customers simply mailed in the entire camera, which was then returned with new film and copies of the photographic prints. For those living in rural areas, the ability to get film developed by mail made photography far more accessible. By transforming its cost and convenience, Eastman made photography widely available to the middle class and, eventually, to most Americans.

You may have heard the phrase "the camera never lies." Since camera use became widespread, photographs have often been treated as recorders of objective and absolute truth (Finnegan, 2001). The American Holocaust Memorial Museum displays thousands of photographs of the Holocaust, not only because they allow visitors to view and understand the events in a different way, but because they provide documentation of the atrocity in a way that makes it difficult to deny. We have long treated photographs as authoritative proof in a variety of circumstances. Photographs are frequently used in criminal trials as proof of guilt or innocence. When you buy products like movies, video games, or alcohol, you may be asked to show a photo I.D. as a way of proving your age. The Internet acronym POIDH ("Pics Or It Didn't Happen") highlights how we are much more likely to believe a story if it is accompanied by photographic proof. After all, seeing is believing.

Yet, after decades of serving as authoritative proof, photographs may be becoming less trustworthy. Photo-editing software such as Adobe Photoshop has made altering images much easier. Perhaps for the first time since photography became widespread, we are now likely to look at an incredible photograph and wonder if it has been manipulated in some way (Pfister and Woods, 2016). One place in which the altering of photographs is particularly common is in advertising, which frequently sells products by displaying images of models that have that have been substantially altered. To see this process in action, find the video "Standard Of Beauty & Photoshop | Model Before and After," posted on YouTube by Global Democracy. Beginning with a relatively average-sized woman as the model, the video displays a number of techniques commonly used by advertisers: The model's eyes and lips are enlarged, her stomach and back are contracted, her legs are elongated, feet shortened, and skin completely retouched. The skincare company Dove displays a number of these same techniques in videos for their Campaign for Real Beauty. Male models receive similar alterations: Men's arms, chests, and shoulders are enlarged, their waists slimmed, their jawlines enhanced, and they are often made taller than women in the image. Some of the image manipulation moves beyond simple photoshopping. For example, Victoria's Secret swimsuit models actually wear pushup bras under their strapless swimsuits in order to create cleavage and then have the entire bra digitally removed from the image (Miller, 2016). If you have ever looked at an image of a model and thought it would be impossible for you to look like that, you might be right—and the model might not look like that either.

Of course, even an unaltered photograph can only tell a partial story. A photograph cannot contain everything, and every photograph reflects particular choices about what to include and what to omit. What gets left out of a photograph can sometimes be more important than what is included. Kevin Deluca and Anne Demo (2000) analyze photographs taken by Carleton Watkins in the 1860s that portray the Yosemite Valley as a pristine place full of lush—and mostly untouched—nature. His beautiful images encouraged tourists to visit and served as the impetus for environmentalists to lobby for governmental protection of the area. Wide circulation of these images played a central role in building political support for the creation of what is now known as Yosemite National Park. Watkins's photographs powerfully reinforced U.S. perceptions of the American West as sublime and untouched precisely because of what they left out: The native people who inhabited that valley for centuries and had been systematically driven out before the pictures were taken. While Watkins's photographs faithfully represent the natural beauty of Yosemite, they also offer a reminder always to ask what has been left out of a photograph.

MOTION PICTURES: MOVIES AND TELEVISION

By the late 1800s, photography had become so widespread that people began experimenting with photographing and depicting an elusive, new subject: motion. Early attempts to capture motion consisted of series of still photographs ordered sequentially and displayed simultaneously. Although photographers had developed the techniques to rapidly photograph a sequence of individual moments, the technologies available to display them were incredibly primitive and often only usable by one viewer at a time. As the technologies to display motion pictures evolved, however, they quickly became central means of visual communication and public entertainment (Dirks, n.d.). The two most important of these media are cinema and television.

CINEMA/MOVIES

While early attempts at displaying motion were often limited to one viewer at a time, the invention of film projectors and the mass production of flexible film reels allowed motion pictures to be displayed onto walls and screens. Rooms, and eventually theaters, full of people could gather and watch a motion picture together. Motion pictures quickly became a popular form of public entertainment. Early theaters called nickelodeons (a combination of the word *nickel* and the Greek word for theater) charged five cents for viewers to watch short films. Just as the Kodak camera had made photography accessible to the middle class, cinema made watching movies affordable to members of the middle and working classes (Sturken and Cartwright, 2009).

TELEVISION

Movies dominated public entertainment from the 1920s to the 1940s. In 1946, 90 million Americans (or 65 percent of the population) went to movie theaters each week. In contrast, there were only 10,000 television sets in the country, few of which were in individual homes. Just a decade later, 15 million American homes had television sets. Today, 27 million Americans (fewer than 10 percent) go to the movies in any given week, but 96.7 percent of American households have televisions.

This transition is significant, because relative to other visual media, television is particularly immersive. We are exposed to it more than most other forms of media. Consider how many hours the average person spends reading a book in a day compared to how many hours they spend watching television. This difference exists in part because of the low level of audience involvement and effort required to consume television. In other words, television viewing is easy and passive. Once a person has turned the television on, it actually takes more effort to turn it off than to just keep watching. This is one reason why the average American watches five hours of television per day.

The Audience's Perception: Cultivation Theory

Television has had profound and complex effects on both individual viewers and our social relations. After conducting several large-scale studies of television viewers, George Gerbner and Larry Gross (1976) developed **cultivation theory**, which suggests that television viewers gradually begin to perceive what they see on television as an accurate representation of the world. For example, television characters are subjected to violence far more than the average person. As a result, Gerbner found that "heavy viewers" who consumed more than four hours of television per day were much more likely to overestimate the amount of violence in the world, to be less trusting of other people, and to feel less comfortable walking alone at night. In addition, heavy television viewers estimated their risk of being victims of violence at ten times that of people who watch less television (Hughes, 1980). These beliefs have political consequences as well: Heavy television viewers tend to support tougher prison sentences and hiring more police officers, which may help explain why the United States leads the developed world in both hours of television watched and incarceration rate.

Of course, believing that television shows accurately represent the world around us can have effects that extend well beyond our perceptions of violence. Television viewing can also affect a viewer's body image and self-esteem. Cultivation theory suggests that the more television we watch, the more we assume that the people we see on television are an accurate reflection of the world. Since television actors are frequently thinner and more attractive than the average person, we often compare ourselves against an unrealistic view of what the average person looks like. As a result, researchers have found that increased television watching correlates with decreased body image (Schooler, Ward, Merriwether, and Carruthers, 2004). Now consider the combination of watching hours of television with the ubiquity of photoshopped models discussed earlier. We increasingly live in a visual communication world in which—whether sitting at home watching television or walking by a magazine stand—we are surrounded by misleading or digitally altered representations of beauty and misleading images of how we should aspire to look.

Political Effects of Television

From the 1950s through the 1970s, television brought Americans together by providing common information to fuel political discussions. Most U.S. television viewers had relatively few viewing options: the three network stations (ABC, NBC, and CBS) and perhaps the publicly funded PBS. At 5:00 P.M., all three network stations broadcast news, leaving television viewers with little choice in what to watch. Because they had relatively little competition, network news programs aimed their programming at general audiences and tried to remain politically neutral enough to appeal to as wide an audience as possible. Coverage on the three channels was relatively similar, and viewers talking about the news would gain relatively similar information regardless of which channel they watched. This provided an important common ground for public deliberation—you and your neighbor might disagree over an issue, but you were likely to agree on which issues were important and your debate would at least be based on similar facts.

This common ground began eroding in the 1980s as cable television became increasingly common. For the first time, a large percentage of television viewers had the option of watching something other than news at 5:00. Those who wanted to watch political news could get it at any time on CNN, while those uninterested in political news could more easily watch entertainment programming. In 1996, political news stations Fox News Channel and MSNBC entered the market. Unlike their predecessors, which aimed to appeal to viewers across the political spectrum, Fox News aimed at capturing conservative viewership and MSNBC soon began trying to capture an audience of liberal viewers (Folkenflik, 2013). By showing the news in a way that confirmed audiences' existing political biases, both stations were quickly able to build audiences with common political orientations. Those audiences—whether they recognize it or not—are choosing to opt out of seeing information that might challenge their existing beliefs, and they are unlikely to even have a common set of facts with which to discuss politics with a neighbor. It is unsurprising that, in the years since cable became a prominent place for Americans to get their news, American politics has become more partisan (*The partisan divide on political values grows even wider*, 2017).

INTERNET AND NEW MEDIA

Perhaps the most important visual communication technology of the past 50 years (or longer) is the Internet. In just half a century—or roughly the time it took printing press technology to move from Germany to England—the

Internet grew from an idea, to a military-funded prototype, to a niche hobby, to an essential part of modern life for over 3.2 billion users. Of course, when we talk about using the Internet, we are really talking about simultaneously using a multitude of different technologies, including computers, microchips, routers, coding, satellites, smart phones, etc. This combination of technologies allows visual content to circulate in ways never before possible.

The core ideas of the Internet were first articulated in the early 1960s by MIT scientists J.C.R. Licklider and Leonard Kleinrock. Licklider proposed connecting a group of computers across the world, while Kleinrock began working out the complex logistics of how to pass information between networked computers (Leiner et al., 2009). These ideas may have been particularly appealing in the 1960s, when the omnipresent threat of nuclear war compelled the U.S. government to consider how to continue governing the country if the Capitol was destroyed. The Department of Defense funded the creation of the ARPANET (Advanced Research Projects Agency Network)—a network of computers that could exchange information across great distances, even if any one of the computers was removed or destroyed. The ARPANET was the first version of what would eventually develop into the modern Internet.

Of course, the ability to send and receive information across great distances at incredible speed has radically transformed how we interact with each other in countless settings. For example, universities have seen major changes to both their academic and social practices. Universities became early hubs of Internet access; much like the printing press, the Internet let scholars exchange ideas more quickly and easily than before. A college student doing research 25 years ago was likely to have physically entered the library, sifted through a physical card catalog, and either been limited to books and journals that were physically in the library or forced to wait weeks to have a source mailed to them from a different library. Today, everyone with a smart phone—whether or not they are affiliated with a university—has access to more information than ever before. You can probably instantly view the majority of your university library's holdings from any computer with an Internet connection.

These technologies have also transformed how students interact on campus. Just 15 years ago, a student moving away to college would likely have had greatly reduced social interactions with their friends from home. Today, visual communication technologies such as Facebook, Instagram, Snapchat, and Face-Time make it easier than ever to regularly see and communicate with friends in a different location. This means fewer students spend their first weeks at college looking to make new friends on campus, choosing instead to communicate with their old friends. Similarly, students can use dating apps to meet people interested in a relationship rather than looking for potential partners on campus. With more than 50 million active users, apps like Tinder expand the dating options far beyond those available to previous generations of students. Moreover, these apps are intensely visual, with users often making snap judgments based on a single photograph.

NEW MEDIA AND INTERACTIVITY

The other visual communication technologies in this chapter combine a variety of past technologies in order to produce a specific type of visual communication (e.g., a printed page, a photograph, a video). The Internet allows for the circulation of all of these. But it is a set of technologies often referred to as "web 2.0" or "new media technologies" that have most radically transformed visual communication in the 21st century. Social media (think Facebook, Twitter, and Snapchat), blogging interfaces (WordPress), and video hosting sites (YouTube) make it easy for any user not just to consume visual content, but also to produce and disseminate media similar to the printing press, the camera, and the motion picture, but with far greater reach and speed. While the printing press allowed cheaper and faster reproduction of written works, the presses themselves were still rare and expensive, and their products were still somewhat bound by geography. Today, anyone with a laptop or smart phone can post an essay on social media that has the capacity to be viewed by millions of users. While cameras have become relatively cheap and easily obtainable, the Internet has made it possible to publish and circulate images among vast audiences. The websites used to display and share images now even include software to alter the images. Apps like Instagram include filters and other tools that allow users to manipulate images prior to posting them to potentially massive audiences. Motion pictures—whether movies or television—were once prohibitively expensive to produce and distribute. Today, technologies such as YouTube have made it possible for users to produce and post videos that are viewed by millions of followers.

Ultimately, these technologies allow users to take a more active role. **Interactivity** refers to how new media technologies enable users to interact with both technology and other users in new ways. You can converse with friends on Snapchat, with members of your campus or local community on a social media page, and with strangers in the comments section of a news story. These technologies also enable new types of interactions with celebrities or political figures. Twitter allows actors like Chris Pratt or Lupita Nyong'o to respond to fans (or hecklers), and comedians like Amy Schumer or Stephen Colbert to joke about banal events in their daily lives. They also allow users to challenge the carefully crafted public image of powerful people or companies in new ways. For example, McDonalds launched the hashtag #McDstories in order for customers to tell positive stories about the company. Twitter users quickly began using the hashtag to make public criticisms of the company for serious issues such as employee wages and the quality of the food, as well as to tell more light-hearted jokes about eating McDonalds while using drugs. These sorts of interactions would have been virtually impossible prior to the new forms of interaction enabled by new media.

POLITICAL EFFECTS OF THE INTERNET

If broadcast television in the 1950s and 1960s gave viewers common facts and stories upon which to engage in political discussion, and cable television disrupted this by allowing viewers to access different sets of information, the Internet is an even greater disruption. The Internet offers an exponentially greater ability to access news that confirms our existing biases or to avoid news at all. Because of the massive amount of information available on the Internet, it is necessary to filter out most of the content we see to find what we are looking for. **Filtering** is the set of active and passive processes by which we select what we do and do not see on the Internet. On a basic level, filtering can be as simple as someone with conservative views visiting the Fox News website rather than the MSNBC site in order to get news that matches their political views, and vice versa. A person might create a Google alert or an RSS (Real Simple Syndication) feed that automatically shows them information that is of interest to them. Most Twitter feeds work in the same way: If you have a Twitter account, you see a customized feed that shows you only posts from a tiny selection of all of the people on Twitter based on who you have chosen to follow. All of the aforementioned examples are the results of active filtering—when you follow or unfollow someone on Twitter, you are making an active choice in what you do or don't want to see.

It is important to remember that much online filtering, however, is passive, and it often happens without your knowledge. When you visit most websites, small files known as cookies get installed on your computer. For example, when you click an advertiser's link on your Facebook newsfeed, Facebook tracks the link you have clicked and those you have ignored. Over time, companies acquire large amounts of information about your interests. By aggregating that data and identifying people with similar interests, companies like Facebook or Amazon can predict with remarkable accuracy the books you are likely to read, products you are likely to buy, and political figures you are likely to support. This allows websites to automatically customize what you see and do not see online based on the preferences of people like you.

The potential political effects of this filtering are substantial. Harvard Professor Cass Sunstein describes the phenomenon as **ideological fragmentation**, when individuals find political information from sources that support their own political beliefs, while avoiding alternative perspectives. Unlike in the broadcast era, the Internet and social media make it possible for conservatives to see only conservative political stories, liberals to see only liberal political stories, libertarians to see only stories with a libertarian slant, etc. This may not necessarily diminish the amount of online political deliberation, but Sunstein claims it diminishes the quality of such debates. Because online political discussions often occur around sources of information (for example, in the comments section of a post), online news sources such as political blogs increase the likelihood of deliberation among only those who already agree. When such discussions occur primarily between those who already hold similar positions and within relatively insular groups, they lead to polarization in which

after deliberation, people are likely to move toward a more extreme point in the direction to which the group's members were originally inclined. With respect to the internet and new communications technologies, the implication is that groups of like-minded people, engaged in discussion with one another, will end up thinking the same thing they thought before—but in more extreme form. (Sunstein, 2007, pp. 60–61)

Conversely, when group members disagree on a topic, group deliberation tends to drive opinions closer to the middle. In other words, viewing political information and then deliberating with others in a group who hold similar views tends to make all members of the group hold those views in much stronger forms, whereas deliberating within a group containing diverse perspectives tends to make all members of the group less extreme in their positions. Extremist groups of all types are driven by precisely this phenomenon—when communicating only with those who agree, extreme positions become both more extreme and seemingly more normal to members of the group. People who seek out political information online tend to already have an existing political ideology, and the Internet allows us to find information that confirms and strengthens that ideology.

For those without a strong interest in politics, filtering also makes it easier than ever to avoid political information entirely. Just as cable provided channels without the 5:00 news, the Internet allows access to endless content that has little to do with politics. Rather than watch or read political programming, viewers can now watch every season of *The Voice* or *The Bachelorette*. Approximately one-third of all of the data sent and received on the Internet comes from the movie streaming service Netflix (Sandvine, 2015). Consider the combination of these aspects of television and the Internet: Users with existing political biases now have the ability to consume exclusively information that strengthens that bias, while those without an interest in politics can easily check out from political information entirely. With the number of truly independent voters steadily decreasing, politicians now have greater incentive to ignore the small pool of swing voters, and instead focus on appealing to their increasingly polarized base. For all of the amazing benefits of the Internet, it also poses major challenges to American democracy.

CONCLUSION

McLuhan recognized that media extend our sense of sight by letting us see things in the world that we otherwise would have been unable to see. Today, it is easy to take for granted that we can view events on the other side of the world with just a few clicks of a keyboard. We may forget that not everyone has the same ability. While the Internet is now available to an ever-growing number of people throughout the world—3.2 billion people now have access to its personal, educational, and commercial benefits—over half of the world's population still does not have this access. This means that many of the world's poorest people are now further disadvantaged whenever they try to compete in an increasingly globalized economy against those who do have Internet access. Numerous charities and social programs have reduced this digital divide, but it remains a tremendous obstacle in many countries (including some rural areas of the United States). Access to books, photographs, television, and the Internet is an increasingly essential part of social mobility throughout the world.

None of these technologies can be fully understood as separate from the broader cultural forces from which they arise. For example, the printing press did not cause the Protestant Reformation, but by allowing the cheap and rapid production of Bibles in different languages, it provided an essential tool that enabled the Reformation to unfold as it did. But the printing press itself was only created because Gutenburg recognized the business potential of fulfilling the existing social desire for cheaper Bibles. And while Gutenburg's research helped improve upon past technologies, one of the main reasons his printing press was so much faster and more influential than its Chinese predecessors was not technological, but cultural: Movable type was much easier to use with Latin-based languages made of twenty-six letters than with Chinese languages comprised of thousands of characters. When exploring visual communication technologies, it is essential to understand the mutual relationship between how technologies influence society and how social forces influence technology. Technologies do not force us to act in one way or another, but they do make us more likely to communicate or act in particular ways by making it easier to do so. By doing so, they shape social forces and give rise to new ways of understanding and interacting with the world.

Predicting the social impacts of any given technology is notoriously difficult, because media users are smart and creative—they turn media to vastly different purposes than those for which they were originally intended or invented. The Internet may have begun as a military technology to enable continued coordination of military forces in the event of a nuclear war and to communicate between universities. Now, millions of people use it to meet people on Tinder and share cat memes. But by paying attention to what types of communication any new technology makes easier, we can better understand the social effects of that technology. This awareness can enable us to be more critical consumers of all types of technology and visual communication.

CHECKLIST: UNDERSTANDING COMMUNICATION TECHNOLOGIES

Imagine a particular technology you use, and consider the following questions:

✓ What types of communication does this technology make faster or easier?

✓ What types of communication does it reduce or replace?

✓ What social connections and groups does this technology make possible?

✓ Who has access to this technology?

✓ What does this technology depict as common or normal?

✓ How does this technology allow things to be bought or sold in new ways?

✓ How is this technology used to market products?

✓ How has what I am seeing been altered?

✓ What is not shown?

4   *Visual Rhetoric*

As we learned in the previous chapter, visual technologies allow new types of organizations to form and new ways of disseminating visual images to emerge. Circulating images across media to reach large numbers of people is particularly important in democratic societies. In a healthy democracy, citizens must discuss and debate matters of shared concern; this deliberation can influence how citizens vote and what policies they support, and even shape how citizens see themselves.

Visual communication plays an important part in this process. The images we consume deeply influence our perceptions of who we are, our understanding of what is happening in the world, and our debates over how we should respond to events large and small. Images such as the trails of smoke floating from the Twin Towers of the World Trade Center on 9/11, civil rights protestors being sprayed with fire hoses, and a World War II–era soldier kissing a nurse in Times Square are just a few that have served as common touchstones from which Americans make sense of the world.

Images also have the potential to cut across news media and provide information that is necessary for a democracy to function. Photographs or videos frequently offer the starting point for numerous conversations about the important news events of the day. The power of the image still stands even if we see different news from our neighbors: When the Internet has made it increasingly easy to consume our news from sources that cater to specific audiences and ideologies, liberal and conservative media outlets may offer conflicting interpretations of what these images mean, but a widely-viewed image can at least provide a common starting point for public discussions.

In addition to bringing audiences together, viewing images enables us to understand and relate to the world in ways that reading about it cannot. To see an image of an event is to become a witness to that event. Photographers and journalists have long recognized the capacity of images to influence viewers. It is one thing to read an article about poverty or a refugee crisis; it is another to see images of hungry children or war-torn neighborhoods. Visual communication scholars study how images can invite multiple and complex reactions from different viewers; these responses may often be "spontaneous and immediate, but just as frequently, of lingering and reflective consideration. Audience engagement with visual rhetoric may reinforce, challenge, or restructure commonly held assumptions and values and may guide individual choices and collective actions" (Olson, Finnegan, and Hope, 2008, p. 3). By presenting information to us in an immediate way, images can shape our understanding and our actions.

This chapter explores some of the central forms visual communication can take in public culture, including iconic images, image events, monuments, and visual propaganda. Whether printed in a newspaper, moving on a screen, or carved into stone, images shape us and call us to work together as a people. They can provide visual metaphors that help us understand complex events by condensing them into a single moment. They can encourage us to reconsider what we thought we knew, or prompt us to imagine new possibilities. They can tell us who we are and which parts of our past are worth remembering. They can elicit strong emotional responses and lead us to identify with or against different groups of people.

ICONIC IMAGES

A small handful of photographs have been particularly prominent and influential in U.S. public culture. Certain images have reached such a level of circulation and public recognition that they become the dominant image by which we visualize a particular historical event. Robert Hariman and John Louis Lucaites

JOE ROSENTHAL/AP Photo

(2007) label these photos **iconic images**, and define them as "photographic images appearing in print, electronic or digital media that are widely recognized and remembered, are understood to be representations of historically significant events, activate strong emotional identification response, and are reproduced across a range of media genres or topics" (p. 27). The authors identify nine iconic images, including, for example, "Migrant Mother," "Times Square Kiss," "Raising the Flag on Iwo Jima," and "Tank Man," the image of a man standing in front of a tank in Tiananmen Square. (A quick Google Image search for any of these titles will bring up the iconic image.) Although the boundaries of which photographs we might consider to be iconic are open to interpretation (every year, many media outlets publish differing lists of "iconic images" from that year), certain images undeniably play a central role in shaping our understanding of ourselves and the world around us.

Part of what makes iconic images iconic is their particularly wide circulation across various media. As mentioned in the introduction, images have the potential to cut across our ideologically-targeted news media. Because of this, they play a particularly important role within a democratic culture by providing a sense of shared experience and offering democratic knowledge. Within a country as large and diffuse as the United States, even significant national events may seem far removed from our daily lives if they occur thousands of miles away. Iconic images position viewers as witnesses to the same significant events and thus create a sense of shared experience amongst a mass audience by ensuring they see those events from the same perspective. Iconic images can also serve as a source of democratic knowledge. By displaying particular citizens engaging in certain types of acts (e.g., a jubilant sailor and nurse kissing at a victory parade in Times Square, or Marines working together to raise the U.S. flag at Iwo Jima), iconic images can suggest to their audience who we are and how we should act as citizens.

One fairly recent example of an iconic image emerged from among the many images that circulated following the 9/11 terrorist attacks. In the immediate aftermath of the attacks, coverage of the events dominated U.S. television, newspapers, and online news media. Much of this coverage came through the circulation of photographs of the attacks and their aftermath at the World Trade Center in New York and at the Pentagon in Washington, D.C. These images included the smoking towers just before their collapse, people jumping from the towers, the rubble on one side of the Pentagon, and a nearly constant repetition of video footage of the towers collapsing. In the days that followed, as Americans sought to make sense of the attacks, other images became prominent. They included rescue workers, long lines of blood donors, reunited family members, and the U.S. flag. These images depicted U.S. resilience in response to the attacks.

From this flood of photographs, one became the iconic image of the moment: Thomas Franklin's photograph of three firefighters raising the U.S. flag at Ground Zero, atop the wreckage of the Twin Towers. Part of its appeal

arose from how it recalled another iconic image, the famous photograph of U.S. Marines raising the flag at Iwo Jima (Hariman and Lucaites, 2007). The visual similarities are striking. Notice (1) how the flagpole cuts a diagonal line across the image, just as in the Iwo Jima image. The firefighters, like the soldiers, (2) stand on a pile of rubble and destruction to raise the American flag. First published in *The Record*, a New Jersey newspaper, the photograph soon appeared on the front page of newspapers across the country and on the cover of special issues of *Time* and *Life* magazines. The scene was reenacted at the 2001 World Series and 2002 Super Bowl. The image has since appeared on numerous collectibles, including plaques, buttons, coffee mugs, silver dollars, and even a postage stamp.

This image, and its subsequent circulation and reappropriation, demonstrate the power of iconic images not just to display what is happening in the world, but also to suggest how we should respond. The raising of the flag represents the same sense of nationalism contained in many of the other flag images circulating at that moment. The firefighters embody many of the same themes represented by Marines in the Iwo Jima photo. They display self-sacrifice in service of the greater purpose represented by the flag above them. They also work together as equals. Notice that (3) it is unclear from the firefighters' position or their uniforms if any of them hold a higher rank than the others; instead, they cooperate to accomplish the labor of raising the flag. The image thus depicts the symbol of the United States, still flying after the attack because of its citizens' commitment to working-class ideals of egalitarian labor and self-sacrifice. In doing so, it redefines the moment "in terms of a still-unrealized victory" (Hariman and Lucaites, 2007, p. 133). It offers a powerful visual metaphor to help viewers make sense of the event and provides viewers guidance on how to perform citizenship in response to current events.

IMAGE EVENTS

An **image event** is a staged action designed to create visual content that can gain widespread circulation and challenge how viewers understand the world. Image events are designed to cut through the tremendous amount of visual content we encounter and grab the attention of large audiences. Simply gaining widespread circulation is not enough. Kevin Deluca (1999) notes that although they are "designed to flag media attention and generate publicity, image events are more than just a means of getting on television. They are crystallized philosophical fragments, mind bombs . . ." (p. 6). In other words, they also work to challenge common understandings and "expand the universe of thinkable thoughts" (Manes, 1990, p. 77). By challenging audiences' assumptions or commonly held beliefs, image events may also induce audience members to reconsider their own relation to the ideas and messages brought forth by the image.

Perhaps the most famous example of an image event was created by members of the environmental organization Greenpeace. Six Greenpeace members followed a fleet of Russian whaling ships in small, inflatable rubber boats and attempted to protect the whales that the Russian fleet was pursuing. As the Russian ship, *Vlastny*, slowed to aim its 90-millimeter canon at a whale, one of the inflatable boats positioned itself just in front of the whale. The Greenpeace activists assumed the Russians would keep sailing rather than risk firing on humans. Instead, the *Vlastny*'s massive cannon fired 160-pound exploding harpoons that passed just over the heads of the Greenpeace activists and killed the whale (Delicath and Deluca, 2003).

Greenpeace activists on the other boats recorded the unexpected exchange. The footage was dramatic. The juxtaposition of the tiny rubber boats standing helplessly against the massive Russian ship, the *Vlastny* crew's disregard for the dangers of firing just over the heads of the Greenpeace activists, and the ease with which the powerful cannon killed the whale all combined to form a striking piece of visual rhetoric. Greenpeace activist Paul Watson—one of the two men on the rubber boat—recognized the potential of this image event to challenge public understanding of whaling, saying "if the public thought about whaling at all, it was the image of Moby Dick that came to mind, along with the brave whaling men in puny longboats locked in a heroic struggle against a monstrous giant beast" (Watson, 2005). The Greenpeace footage completely undermined this common perception of whaling and confronted viewers with the industrial power and raw violence of contemporary whaling. The footage was aired repeatedly on U.S. network news and throughout the world, generated widespread dialogue, and contributed to the passing of legislation restricting commercial whaling.

The creation of image events has become an increasingly common part of social movements. They offer a particularly powerful tactic to marginalized groups or those seeking to take on better funded or more powerful opposition. Protest groups may not have the resources to engage in protest and direct action every day. They rarely have financial resources equal to the corporations or governments they challenge. By creating image events, these groups are able to manufacture visual communication that continues to circulate and reach broad audiences long after the activists have returned home. Social media have offered increased possibilities for image events, by making it possible for images or videos to "go viral," even without the assistance of traditional news media. Occasionally, an image or video may garner so much circulation on social media that traditional news media outlets begin covering it. By intentionally creating image events designed to circulate via both news media and social media, activists can reach a wide audience and challenge them to envision the world in new ways.

MONUMENTS AND PUBLIC MEMORY

Photographs and video footage are not the only types of visual communication that help us identify and act together as a group. **Monuments** and memorials are visual representations of the past that provide viewers with important cues about who we are and which people and events from our past are worthy of remembrance and emulation. Unlike other forms of visual communication that can be easily reproduced and disseminated across great distances, monuments tend to occupy important—even sacred—spaces. Rather than seeing them on social media or in line at a grocery counter, we make special trips to view them. Whether located at the sites of significant events (often where people have died) or at dedicated spaces of remembrance (such as the Washington Mall), their presence on sacred space imbues monuments with unique authority to interpret the past. Roy Rosenzweig and David Thelen (1998) interviewed 1,500 Americans who visited historical and memorial sites and found that visitors to such sites believed them to offer more accurate accounts of the past than other records such as eye-witness accounts, newspaper articles, and history books. As such, how the past is visually represented at memorial sites plays an important role in how we remember it.

Yet, no monument can objectively represent the past. What we choose to remember about the past and whose version of history gets carved into stone make monuments intensely political. Just as any photograph represents a photographer's decision about what is worth recording, monuments and memorials tend to reflect very specific—and often very contentious—decisions about which people and events from the past are worth remembering and celebrating. The stakes of such decisions are high, as those representations of the past "that are actually made . . . come to be seen as important, correct, normal and so forth. That renders their far more numerous unmaterialized counterparts as perhaps not so important, correct, or normal" (Blair, Dickinson, and Ott, 2010, p. 4). Every monument represents a choice to recognize some people and perspectives in lieu of others. By choosing certain things over others as worthy of remembrance, monuments present particular arguments about who we are, how we should remember the past, and how we should act in the future.

The Vietnam Veterans Memorial (VVM) in Washington, D.C., offered one of the most well-known and fascinating disputes over how to visually represent the past. The VVM, nestled in the Constitutional Gardens at the foot of the Lincoln Memorial, is one of the best known memorials in the country. While much of the Washington Mall is filled with chatting tourists and running children, the VVM almost always feels quiet, calm, and contemplative. The disputes over how to represent the war were just the opposite.

After a group of veterans raised money and lobbied Congress and the National Park Service to secure the memorial a site on the National Mall, they issued a call for designs for a memorial that would "(1) be reflective and contemplative in character; (2) harmonize with its surroundings; (3) contain the names of those who had died in the conflict or who were still missing; and (4) make no political statement about the war" (Fish, 1987, p. 3). The winner of

Courtesy of Ryan McGeough

the contest was designer Maya Lin's now iconic black granite wall. Set into the earth, the wall extends nearly 500 feet and contains the names of 58,307 men and women who died or went missing in the conflict. Next to each name of the fallen appears a diamond; next to the names of the Missing-In-Action (MIA) appear a small cross, which is changed into a diamond if the soldier is found dead. If the MIA soldier returns, the cross would be carved into a circle; no such engraving has yet been necessary (Sturken, 1997, p. 46). When viewers look at the names, they also see their own reflection in the polished granite. Visitors to the wall frequently find particular names, touch them, reproduce the names on sheets of paper by rubbing a crayon or pencil over the name, or leave personalized artifacts and letters under specific names.

Despite the beauty of the wall, its representation of the Vietnam War made it immensely controversial (McGeough, 2011). Visually, the low, black wall, carved into a hillside, offers a stark contrast to virtually all of the other monuments and memorials at the mall. Indeed, it is hard to imagine a monument more different in appearance from the nearby Washington Monument: a 554-foot white tower celebrating the nation's first president. As a result, many influential politicians and donors publically opposed the monument. They labeled it a "black gash of shame" (as cited in Scruggs and Swerdlow, 1985, pp. 81–82) and described it as disrespectful to veterans. These opponents saw the list of names as a visual representation of the costs of the war without any recognition of what the troops were fighting for. Eventually, supporters and opponents compromised by adding

Courtesy of Ryan McGeough

another element to the memorial: a sculpture of three soldiers along with an American flag. The eight-foot sculpture, designed by Frederick Hart and entitled *Three Soldiers*, offers a realist representation of three soldiers of different races standing together with their weapons in hand or over their shoulder. The new addition to the site offered a profoundly different visual representation of the war. Its depiction of masculine camaraderie and inclusion of the flag highlight why many veterans fought.

This new choice about how to visually represent the past caused yet another controversy. Women who had served in the conflict found their perspective absent from the memorial site. The founder of the Vietnam Women's Memorial Project, Diane Carlson Evans, claims that "the wall in itself was enough, but when they added the men, it became necessary to add women to complete the memorial" (as quoted in Forgery, 1991, September 20, p. 18). They believed the wall alone, which contains the names of the eight women killed in the war, represented women equally. But the addition of Hart's decidedly masculine statue visualized veterans' experiences in a way that did not reflect the 11,500 female nurses who served during the conflict. Eleven years after the dedication of the VVM, the Vietnam Women's Memorial was unveiled. Created by Glenna Goodacre, it depicts an injured and blindfolded male soldier being tended to by a white female nurse, an African American female nurse staring up into the sky, and a third female nurse kneeling over a crate of medical supplies. Stylistically, the Women's Memorial parallels *Three Soldiers*. It supplements Hart's representation

Courtesy of Ryan McGeough

of masculine heroism with a depiction of the suffering, confusion, and perpetual contact with death experienced by many female Vietnam veterans.

The Wall, *Three Soldiers*, and The Vietnam Women's Memorial all reflect the same war. But their starkly different decisions about how to visually represent the conflict draw the attention of visitors toward very different aspects of it. The black wall displays the tremendous costs of the war. By presenting the names of the fallen in chronological order of their deaths—rather than by alphabetical order—it offers a time line of the sacrifices of the war. *Three Soldiers* visualizes the war in more traditional form. It depicts the experiences of infantrymen and seeks to display why veterans fought by celebrating the brotherhood of those who fought together and displaying a flag. The Vietnam Women's Memorial represents the often ignored experiences of the women who served. No one of these representations is more "right" or historically accurate than the others. But these different visual representations encourage visitors to remember very different versions of the war. Whether highlighting the costs of war or celebrating the reasons soldiers fought, the different memorials offer very different lessons for visitors considering whether the United States should go to war in the future.

PROPAGANDA

When you think of propaganda, what comes to mind? For most people, the term has negative connotations. You may imagine state-controlled media glorifying a dictator. This is certainly one form propaganda frequently takes. **Propaganda** is the use of art to create an emotional response in audience members and lead them to particular political identifications. It often presents simplified, misleading, or even false information in order to get viewers to think or act in a specific way (Lester, 2014). Propaganda's negative connotations come from both its aim of manipulating people, as well as its association with numerous dictators who have relied on propaganda to gain or hold power.

Perhaps the best-known propaganda film in history is *Triumph of the Will*. The 1935 film, directed by Leni Riefenstahl and co-produced with Adolph Hitler, depicts an actual Nazi rally in Nuremberg. Using what was then cutting-edge cinematography—such as aerial photography and multiple, moving cameras—the film depicts Hitler as the unquestioned leader of a powerful army and unified people. It begins with footage of Hitler's plane flying over Nuremburg as crowds gather to cheer his arrival. He appears as a messianic figure, descending from the clouds to save a people who await his arrival. The film then portrays a four-day rally. Hitler is shown giving speeches each day to large groups of workers, children, and soldiers. The cameras oscillate between the crowd's perspective and Hitler's. From the lower camera angle of the crowd's perspective, Hitler stands as a towering and powerful presence. When shot from Hitler's perspective, the footage consistently emphasizes the massive crowds cheering his every statement. Throughout the speeches depicted in the film, few problems or policies are presented. There is no explicit anti-Semitism and only vague references to dishonesty in the press and corruption in the leadership. Rather, Hitler promises to unify Germany as the leader of its rebirth. Both visually and in statements such as "the people have joined and justified this leadership" (Riefenstahl, 1935), the film depicts Hitler as a strong man who embodies the hopes of his followers and nation, and who calls viewers to join his movement.

Today, visual propaganda is increasingly common. Producing it no longer requires large budgets or substantial video equipment. Cheap digital cameras and photo-editing software, along with easy online dissemination, have made it easy for even poorly funded extremist groups and their supporters to produce and distribute visual propaganda (Dauber, 2014). Propaganda videos were amongst the earliest and most effective recruiting tools for the jihadist organization, ISIS. Despite often using grainy footage from cell-phone cameras and depicting suicide bombings, these propaganda videos follow the same basic dramatic structure you might expect to find in any movie or television program: The characters and conflict are introduced, the mission begins, the action reaches its climax as the bombing is completed, and the viewer is offered catharsis by being told the suicide bomber has become a celebrated martyr. In some of the videos, attacks on secular targets are digitally edited to include religious symbols. Raw footage of the event shows an old van detonating in front of a poorly marked, concrete police station; the propaganda videos feature editing and animation that replace the van with a shining 18-wheeler flying an ISIS flag or digitally add crosses to their targets. The videos intentionally avoid representing the multiple and complex tensions between various groups in contemporary Iraq. Instead, they attempt to frame the conflict simplistically as a holy war between Islam and Christianity (Perry and Long, 2015). This framing ignores tensions within Islam, Muslim resistance to ISIS, and even the Iraqis killed in the attacks. Instead, the videos attempt to visually represent ISIS as the champions of Islam and call other Muslims to join them.

Propaganda is not just a tool of foreign dictators, nor must it only be used in service of oppressive regimes or ideologies. Democratically elected governments also produce propaganda. Shortly after the attacks on Pearl Harbor, the U.S. government commissioned seven propaganda films entitled *Why We Fight*. The films were used to convince both soldiers and citizens of the importance of U.S. participation in the war, after years of commitment to not intervening in foreign conflicts. They depict the conflict in simple and stark contrasts: Producer Frank Capra (1971) aimed to create "a general picture of two worlds, the slave and the free" (p. 335). Later films show British and Russian soldiers heroically defending their homeland against an enemy bent on enslaving them. These representations of the Allies and Axis cast the conflict in simplified terms of good versus evil, freedom versus slavery, and support of or opposition to "traditional values." They left out important details about Russian human rights violations in order to unify American support for the war. Yet, almost as soon as the war ended, the details left out of *Why We Fight* became the justification for U.S. propaganda vilifying the Russians.

Most contemporary political advertisements include elements of propaganda. Consider the famous "Yes, We Can" video that was released during then-Senator Barack Obama's 2008 presidential campaign. Although it was not originally produced by the campaign, the video received over 22 million views within a month, was added to Obama's campaign website, and was such a success that will.i.am and John Legend were invited to perform the song at the Democratic National Convention later that year. The video features footage taken from Obama's concession speech after losing the New Hampshire primary to Hillary Clinton. Obama's statements are put to music and accompanied by a variety of celebrities including will.i.am, Scarlett Johannsen, Enrique Murciano, and John Legend. The video includes statements such as "It was a creed written into the founding documents that declared the destiny of a nation. Yes, we can. . . . Yes, we can to opportunity and prosperity. Yes, we can to heal this nation. Yes, we can to repair this world. Yes, we can." Although Obama's original speech contains a variety of policy proposals, the lines selected for the video do not. Like most political advertisements, it focuses less on specific policies and more on general ideals that viewers are likely to share. Aligning a candidate with opportunity and prosperity is certainly easier than engaging the tricky questions of how to best create them. Particularly to the young voters who played an important role in Obama's election, the video displays an attractive community to identify with: a young, successful, good-looking, and ethnically-diverse group of supporters rallying behind a leader committed to healing the nation and repairing the world. The next time you see a political advertisement, pay attention to whether it focuses on the merits of a particular candidate's policies or on creating an emotional identification with a particular group. Despite its negative connotations, propaganda is a regular component of contemporary politics and a common part of our lives.

CHECKLIST: UNDERSTANDING VISUAL RHETORIC

Select an image you think is a type of visual rhetoric discussed in this chapter. Then, answer the questions below.

✓ How widely is this image likely to be viewed?

✓ Who is likely to view this image?

✓ How does the image represent what is occurring in the world?

✓ How does it challenge or reaffirm our assumptions about the subject it depicts?

✓ Is this image likely to create an emotional response in most viewers?

✓ Who or what is included in this image?

✓ Who or what is left out?

✓ Does the image tell us something about who we are as a community?

✓ What does it suggest is most important to remember?

✓ How does the image simplify what it depicts?

✓ Does the image encourage us to identify with certain people or causes?

ANALYZING VISUAL RHETORIC

This photograph almost instantly became an iconic image. In isolation, it is engrossing. Even if you know nothing about its context, the composition of the photograph makes it striking. The woman in the photograph, Ieshia Evans, appears to be standing still. As she stands, straight and dignified, her sundress billows in the breeze and the two officers in riot armor rush toward her. A few onlookers and photographers stand scattered in the background behind Evans; behind the officers stands a row of officers in formation.

JONATHAN BACHMAN/REUTERS/Newscom

You can see many of the elements of design from Chapter 2 in this photograph. Notice (1) how the crack in the road creates a vertical line running down the center of the image between Evans and the police. You automatically recognize the (2) implied movement of the oncoming officers because of the diagonal lines of their legs, but perceive Evans as stationary. The close proximity and similarity of the two officers' uniforms lead you to interpret them as working together and (3) as part of a group with the other officers behind them. Evans, by contrast, appears alone.

Yet, these elements only tell part of the story. To understand why this photograph became arguably the most iconic image of 2016, you also need to know its context. Photographer Jonathan Bachman took this photograph on July 9, 2016, in Baton Rouge, Louisiana, at a protest against police using excessive violence against African American men. The protest was prompted by the death of Alton Sterling, a 37-year-old African American man who had been killed by police officers in Baton Rouge on July 5. On July 6, Philandro Castille, an African American man in Minnesota, was shot by police while reaching for his wallet. On July 7, at a protest in Dallas in which police and protestors had been interacting peacefully, a sniper opened fire and killed five officers. By the time of the Baton Rouge protest, tensions were high.

Against this backdrop of excessive violence, the photo of Evans becomes particularly powerful. The image encapsulates the events of the previous week through a visual metaphor of overreaction: a peaceful African American woman in a sundress, simultaneously vulnerable and defiant, swarmed by two white officers wearing layers of riot armor. The officers' equipment suggests they came prepared for violent resistance like that in Dallas. Instead, the photograph captures only Evans's quiet and unthreatening act of protest. The image focuses on Evans, leaving out the other protestors who stand further back on the road. It challenges public representations of protestors as violent, instead depicting the current moment in a way that hearkens back to images of nonviolent resistance from the American Civil Rights movement.

It also suggests a potentially unbridgeable divide between the white officers and the African American protestor—one so deep it is even reflected in the pavement. In contrast to many famous images from the Civil Rights movement, both Evans's and the officers' faces lack emotion. Neither Evans nor the officers appear angry or afraid. Evans submits without resisting. The angle of the two officers suggests they are trying to slow down before reaching her, to arrest her without harming her. There is something almost frighteningly mechanical about the scene: Both Evans and the officers perform their roles without joy or anger, dutifully playing their parts within a larger social drama beyond their control. It is unsurprising that this image became iconic at a moment in which public attention began to focus on how to stop the previous week's cycle of violence.

5   *Visual Culture*

The term **visual culture** can refer to cultures in which visual media are ubiquitous and viewing visual media is central to how individuals and groups understand themselves and the world. The term actually has dozens of published definitions: Some focus on the cultures themselves, while others define visual culture as the academic study of such cultures. Throughout this book, we have considered many of the key components of visual culture. We have explored the ubiquity of images, their tendency to reference past images, the various building blocks by which visuals are created, how technologies shape image production and consumption, and the role of visual communication in public culture.

This chapter focuses on cultural aspects of the often interrelated processes through which we interpret and produce visual communication. Of course, these processes are intertwined: A clearer understanding of how we interpret visual communication can help you more effectively produce visual communication, and understanding more about how visual meaning is produced can help you be a savvier consumer of visual communication.

INTERPRETING VISUAL COMMUNICATION

To understand how we interpret visual communication, we can look to **semiotics**, the study of signs. The contemporary study of how signs take on and communicate their meaning began with American pragmatist philosopher Charles Sanders Peirce, who, along with Swiss linguist Ferdinand de Saussure, developed the field of semiotics. Both were primarily focused on words as signs, but French philosopher Roland Barthes, who studied topics ranging from photography to professional wrestling, helped bring the ideas of semiotics to the analysis of visual symbols (Chandler, 1994).

THREE TYPES OF SIGNS

Peirce identified three types of signs: *iconic, indexical*, and *symbolic*. Each type of sign is based upon its relationship to the thing it signifies, and the three types of signs communicate meaning based on "qualities, existential facts, or conventions," respectively (Atkin, 2013). Peirce believed that the object being signified determined the appropriate sign. In other words, some objects demand iconic signs, while others require symbolic signs.

Iconic signs resemble the objects they represent (also known as the *referent*). They depict some recognizable quality of their referent. For example, in order to alert you to the possibility of pedestrians crossing the street, a road sign may depict people walking in a crosswalk. As long as an iconic sign sufficiently depicts some essential characteristics of what it represents, most viewers are likely to understand it. Even a young child's crayon drawing of a dog may bear enough resemblance to make you think of a dog. Because of the direct resemblance of the sign to the referent, iconic signs tend to be the easiest to decode.

Indexical signs draw upon some type of physical or existential relationship between the sign and the referent. If two things tend to exist together or accompany one another, one may be used as a sign of the other. For example, a photograph depicting thick smoke rising from a forest can represent a forest fire—even if the flames themselves are not visible in the photograph. In this example, the common phrase "where there's smoke, there's fire" summarizes the indexical relationship: We see smoke and logically interpret it as a sign of something we have learned accompanies smoke. Indexical signs may be less direct: You might see an image of a woman with a stethoscope and assume she is a doctor, or a child with a thermometer in his mouth and assume he is ill. This connection is less automatic than an iconic sign; our ability to interpret indexical signs comes from our lived experiences of observing things that tend to accompany one another.

Symbolic signs gain their meaning through learned social conventions. Unlike iconic signs that resemble their referent, or indexical signs that bear a logical and learned relationship with their referent, symbolic signs have no necessary relationship to what they represent. The connection between them is arbitrary and constructed within a particular symbol system. The use of a red octagon as a sign to stop is almost universally understood by Americans. This same sign holds no meaning in many other countries, where triangles are frequently associated with stop signs. That is because these are symbolic signs, and Americans grow up being taught a specific way to interpret and respond to red octagons. Words typically function as symbolic signs. For example, no obvious or necessary relationship exists between the word *tree* and the object of a tree. When referring to abstract concepts, the relationship is even less obvious: There is certainly no necessary relationship between the word *sale* and the idea that the products in a store will be sold at a lower price than usual. Because of the lack of a direct connection between symbolic signs and the things they signify, the meaning of symbolic signs must be taught.

As Peirce recognized, some referents (like people crossing in a crosswalk) are most efficiently communicated through iconic symbols. Others (like jealousy or fear) are most easily represented through symbolic signs. We often combine different types of signs into a single visual image. For example, most U.S. airplane bathrooms have *No Smoking* signs depicting a cigarette in a red circle with a slash through it. The image of a cigarette functions as an iconic sign: It resembles the object of a cigarette. The red circle with a slash through it functions as a symbolic sign: We have to learn that it means *no* or *do not*. Once we understand the symbolic meaning of the circle and slash, we can then make sense of this common visual symbol. Though not universal, the circle and slash symbol is among the most widely recognized symbolic signs. As such it communicates its meaning across a wide variety of language barriers. However, most symbolic signs only function within a relatively limited community who have been taught how to interpret them.

DECODING IMAGES

The process by which we learn to read images, and especially symbolic signs, is often more complex than someone simply telling us what a particular sign means. Any given sign may have both connotative and denotative meanings. A sign's **denotative meaning** is a widely agreed-upon meaning that it holds within a particular community. However, even if a sign has a meaning that is universally recognized within a community, viewers may associate many other meanings with it as well. A symbol's **connotative meaning** is the variety of meanings, attitudes, and emotions that viewers associate with it. Words often have clear denotative meanings; you can look up their definitions in a dictionary. Defining images is trickier. Because it is hard to define the denotative meaning of an image, connotations play a particularly essential role in assigning meaning to visual communication (Barthes, 1977).

Even simple visual symbols are often loaded with a variety of connotations. Consider the swastika: What does it mean? What does it make you think of? Imagine you saw someone with a swastika tattoo; what judgments might you make about that person? For most viewers in Europe and the Americas, this relatively simple combination of lines evokes immensely negative connotations. Some American viewers may see it and think of the Holocaust. Others may think of Nazism, neo-Nazism, or contemporary racism. Still others may think of family members or ancestors who fought in World War II and died or were wounded. Throughout the Western world, the swastika is highly stigmatized due to its various associations with Nazism. In contemporary Germany and many other countries throughout Europe and South America, public displays of the swastika are illegal. However, this same symbol evokes profoundly different connotations in other places. The swastika is an important symbol in many Eastern religions including Hinduism, Jainism, and Buddhism. To followers of these religions, or members of cultures in which the swastika is prominently displayed as a religious symbol, it may have a variety of connotations entirely different from how those in the West interpret it. This highlights two important aspects of how we interpret the visual media we consume: First, how a viewer interprets an image is influenced by that viewer's culture. Second, the fact that viewers may interpret and respond to a symbol in multiple ways suggests that the meaning of any image is not controlled only by its creator.

The question of how culture affects our understanding of symbols is complex. Cultural studies scholar Stuart Hall (1993) argues that any culture in which a message is produced has an elaborate system of coded connotations and meanings that influence how that message is interpreted by an audience. These "codes" range from an audience's simple understanding of symbolic signs (such as the ability to understand words) to complex ideological values (such as the belief that Communism is bad). However, Hall recognizes that audience members are not just passive receivers; rather, they play an active and important role in "decoding" messages. Hall argues that a viewer may adopt one of three positions when interpreting a message.

1. A *dominant reading*: The audience member understands the codes of the text and accepts the creator's preferred reading.

2. A *negotiated reading*: The audience member largely accepts the preferred reading of the text, but recognizes possible exceptions (usually due to personal experiences or interests).

3. An *oppositional reading*: The audience member understands the preferred meaning and connotations of a text, but chooses to actively reject them. An oppositional reading generally occurs when an audience member views a text through an alternate set of codes and assumptions.

Hall's three audience positions can be easily illustrated through political campaign advertisements. For example, during the 2016 presidential primary, Donald Trump's first televised campaign advertisement focused on immigration and terrorism. The ad depicts footage first of a group of people all stuck on one side of a wall and then of a large group of immigrants rushing across a border without a wall, as the narrator announces Trump's plan to "stop illegal immigration by building a wall on our southern border that Mexico will pay for." The ad was widely discussed in the national news media, and it was simultaneously well received by Trump's supporters and highly criticized by his opponents. A dominant reading of this advertisement might focus on the word *illegal*, the footage of immigrants rushing across the border, and the statement that "Mexico will pay for" the wall. Someone adopting a dominant reading might reach the preferred conclusion that Trump's policy would be effective and necessary. A negotiated reading of the same advertisement might focus on the same words and images, and also share a belief that illegal immigration is a problem and building a wall might be effective. However, such a viewer might also consider that they work or attend classes with someone who immigrated illegally or overstayed their visa, and believe that person is different from other immigrants and deserves to stay in the United States. Negotiated readings often entail contradictions between a viewer's acceptance of a general belief or ideology and specific exceptions from their own experiences. An oppositional reading would reject the assumptions of the advertisement. A viewer engaged in an oppositional reading might believe that the United States is a nation of immigrants and that attempts to focus on immigration from Mexico rather than Canada are thinly-veiled racism. An oppositional reader approaches the advertisement from a completely different set of ideological assumptions, and thus is unlikely to adopt the creator's preferred meaning. Any text may be read in different ways by different audiences.

PRODUCING VISUAL COMMUNICATION

In Chapter 2, we explored the building blocks of visual design that might be used to create an image or advertisement. This section focuses on how visual symbols can be imbued with meaning, as well as how existing meanings might be challenged or changed.

FRAMING IMAGES WITH WORDS

Hall notes that the meaning of a text is created through a variety of factors, including the author encoding the ideas, the actual text that is created, and how viewers make sense of that text. Because audiences play an active role in interpretation, any text is likely to provoke a range of interpretations (some of which are opposed to what the creator intended). This demonstrates not only that a text does not have just one meaning, but also that the creator of a text does not have absolute control over how it will be interpreted. Remember that this is particularly true of visual images, given their reliance on connotative meaning. Think back to the example of the Vietnam Veterans' Memorial from the previous chapter. The Wall's creator, Maya Lin, believed she was avoiding an explicitly political message while displaying the names of the fallen. Her opponents believed that the black stone wall was disrespectful to those who died. Who was right? What did the Wall mean? What did the statue of the *Three Soldiers* mean? How can you be sure?

   The fact that viewers might have different responses to the same symbol does not mean that you cannot influence how your visual communication is interpreted or make viewers more likely to interpret a message in the way you intended. It is important to consider your target audience and how you might guide their interpretations when creating any sort of visual text. One important way that producers of images help viewers interpret them is by framing the images with words (McGeough and McGeough, 2014). This might range from providing pages of context and explicit instructions for what to notice about an image (as I have occasionally provided throughout this book) to a simple caption under a newspaper photograph. You can never be absolutely sure a visual text will be interpreted as you intend, but providing accompanying text can offer interpretive clues that make some interpretations more likely than others.

   Look at this anti-smoking advertisement (Figure 5.1). Without reading the text, what do you think it is trying to communicate? The image depicts (1) a

Figure 5.1

pack of cigarettes in which (2) each cigarette is wrapped in the paper that typically surrounds crayons. You can probably assume that it is about smoking and children. If you saw this in an American magazine and were aware of American taboos around smoking, you could probably predict that the advertisement was anti-smoking. But without the accompanying text, it is difficult to tell much more. Now look at the text. The words "Just like mommy" appear in crayon (3), and below them is the statistic "Children whose parents or siblings smoke are three times more likely to smoke than children living in non-smoking homes." Does this help the unusual image make more sense? Here, the text and image complement one another. The text guides your interpretation of the images, and the images (both of the pack of cigarettes and the writing in crayon) add an emotional power that makes the statistic more compelling.

Often, words provide information without which the same image would be interpreted in radically different—and even opposite—ways. One particularly famous example of this occurred after Hurricane Katrina devastated New Orleans. In the aftermath of the storm, which caused over 1800 casualties and destroyed large areas of the city, the Associated Press and Getty Images released the following two photographs of seemingly similar events. The pair of images appeared together on Yahoo! News and sparked immediate outrage across a variety of media outlets. Look at each image: What do you see? How are they similar? How do they differ? Can you see why they created a controversy?

Figure 5.2

Figure 5.3

Although the actions depicted in the images look very similar, the captions describe them differently. The caption of the AP image in Figure 5.2 describes its subject as "looting a grocery store," while the caption of the second image in Figure 5.3 describes its subjects as "finding bread and soda from a local grocery store." Did you notice the other difference? The individual described as "looting" is African American, and the couple who "found bread and soda" are

white. Although both news services defended their choice of captions as techni-
cally correct descriptions of the contents of the photographs, many people were
unhappy with how the words with which each image was captioned encouraged
viewers to interpret similar images of comparable actions by black and white
hurricane survivors in very different ways.

ALTERING SYMBOLS

Resignification is the process by which the cultural connotations or uses of a
symbol are altered. Words frequently undergo resignification. Symbols like the
word *queer* originated as terms of identification gay men used to identify themselves. Over time, the term took on a pejorative connotation as the term was
used as a homophobic insult. More recently, LGBT people have actively worked
to reclaim the term as positive; as a result, you are now likely to hear people
use the term in a positive way (Butler, 1993; Palczewski, Ice, and Fritch, 2016).
Although the process of resignifying a symbol is typically slow and gradual—
using a symbol in a new way does not immediately change how others use or
understand it—the connotations and uses of symbols can change over time.

Resignification can sometimes result from a long and sustained campaign to
challenge and change how a symbol is interpreted. But symbols can also be resignified by simply using them in a new way, using them in contexts that alter their
connotations, or using them in combination with different symbols. Because so
much of the meaning of images comes from their connotations, creating new
associations can quickly change how they are understood within a culture. Consider sculptor Arturo Di Modica's famous sculpture, *Charging Bull* (Figure 5.4).

Figure 5.4

As the title suggests, the massive sculpture depicts a bull (a commonly used metaphor for economic growth) and has become a well-known landmark near the New York Stock Exchange in the financial district of Manhattan. Di Modica created the statue as a tribute to economic optimism after the stock market crashed in 1987. This sculpture stood—relatively unchanged—in its current location near Wall Street since 1990, becoming a popular tourist stop and symbol of American capitalism and economic growth.

Over time, both new cultural connotations and association with new symbols have resignified *Charging Bull*. In the aftermath of the 2008 financial crisis, public anger about the economic collapse was largely directed at Wall Street stock traders and financial institutions. For some, *Charging Bull* served as a visual representation of their unchecked greed. When the 2011 Occupy Wall Street protests began, barriers had to be placed around the sculpture to prevent it from being vandalized by anti–Wall Street protesters. Then, in 2017, a second sculpture was installed nearby. *Fearless Girl*, created by artist Kristen Visbal, depicts a young girl in a dress and high-top shoes with her hands on her hips. Since the second sculpture is placed directly across from *Charging Bull*, it is difficult to view the two sculptures as separate pieces of art. Instead, a viewer sees the four-foot-tall girl standing defiantly in front of the eleven-foot-tall bull. The visually powerful juxtaposition transforms how viewers are likely to interpret both symbols. Rather than being a sign of economic growth, the bull becomes a fearsome antagonist. The brave girl stares down the symbol of American capitalism. The resignification is so powerful that Di Modica threatened to sue to have *Fearless Girl* removed, claiming it violated copyright laws by using and altering the meaning of his sculpture. *Charging Bull* itself remains physically unchanged, but changing attitudes toward Wall Street and the addition of *Fearless Girl* reveal how new connotations and associations with new symbols can powerfully and immediately resignify an existing symbol.

MEMES

Often, when we think of memes, we envision those easy-to-caption pictures of Willy Wonka on Facebook. The term *meme,* however, can also be understood as a way of describing how a text or piece of information spreads from person to person, and this term is much older than the memes we often think of now. The term originates from Richard Dawkins's 1976 book *The Selfish Gene,* in which he claims, "We need a name for the new replicator, a noun which conveys the idea of a unit of cultural transmission, or a unit of imitation" (p. 208). He offers the word *meme,* based in the root word *mimesis,* the classical Greek word for imitation. Dawkins argues that cultural information functions similarly to genes, the genetic information that passes from generation to generation. Cultural information replicates, it is modified and adapted over time, and some information becomes dominant and widespread while some fades away. The comparison may seem odd at first, but the meme/gene similarities are strong enough that they probably shape how you talk about how information spreads on the Internet in ways you take for granted. Consider another biological organism that transmits its genetic information in a similar way: the virus. When a meme suddenly becomes ubiquitous, we describe it as "going viral."

Unlike genes and viruses, however, alteration of memes is not an accident or deviation from the norm. Memes are constantly modified, as the people who create and circulate them tap into existing social knowledge and visual tropes as a way to disseminate a message. Hashtags provide an example of a type of meme that does just that: Twitter marks a hashtag as "trending" when many users post it in a short period of time. Although each of those users may post the same hashtag, they also include a wide variety of information (whether created by themselves or reposted from others) along with the hashtag. Neither the specific hashtag nor even the individual post containing it can be fully understood without reference to the broader set of posts containing the hashtag. Recall the #McDstories example from Chapter 3. Neither the symbol #McDstories, nor any one of the individual posts containing it, is particularly meaningful on its own. However, the hashtag was a meme that allowed many individual users to form a community around telling a variety of personal stories. These stories were widely disseminated and viewed together to form and participate in a broader narrative (see Kennerly and Pfister, 2018).

When a meme is widely adopted, it allows information—often visual symbols—to spread quickly. Think about your own experience with memes. You likely have seen, and perhaps posted, several memes that have gone viral. Some images go viral in short, intense bursts. For example, in February 2015, a woman posted a picture of a dress on the Internet discussion board Reddit. She asked viewers to identify its colors to determine whether it was blue and black or white and gold. Within 48 hours, the post had 400,000 comments, while a Buzzfeed poll on the dress received over 1.8 million responses in just 10 hours. Within a week, the poll had over 28 million views and public figures ranging from Taylor Swift and Kim Kardashian West to U.S. Senator Christopher Murphy had offered their opinions via social media (Mahler, 2015). International media outlets ran stories on the dress. Then, almost as quickly, the phenomenon passed.

Others memes seem to reappear consistently across time. Today, the term *meme* often connotes captionable images, also known as *image macros*, which allow users to add captions to existing images or share images captioned by others. Such memes are captioned and circulated for a wide variety of purposes. Some, such as the Grumpy Cat or Pun Dog memes, tend to circulate as primarily apolitical humor. Others, such as the Condescending Willy Wonka meme or the multitude of "Facepalm" memes frequently contain some sort of cultural or political criticism. Still others, such as the Pepe the Frog meme (Figure 5.5) are most known for being intensely political.

The Pepe the Frog meme provides a fascinating example of how memes blur the lines of authorship and how images can be resignified in ways that move well beyond the intentions of the original creator. Pepe the Frog originated as a cartoon frog drawn by artist Matt Furie and published in the 2006 comic series, *Boy's Club*. A specific image of Pepe saying "feels good man" began

Figure 5.5

going viral in 2008 as users posted the image and catchphrase. The meme continued to spread as users created images of Pepe in a wide variety of situations; in 2014 Katy Perry posted a picture of Pepe crying in a Tweet about having jet lag. The meme began taking on different connotations, however, as users on Reddit and 4chan (the site where Pepe first went viral) decided to "reclaim" Pepe from his wider use in pop culture. They began creating a series of racist and anti-Semitic images using variations of the Pepe meme. Some altered the text to say things like "Kill Jews Man," while others altered the image of Pepe to portray the frog with a Hitler-style moustache or dressed in a Ku Klux Klan robe. These racist versions of the Pepe meme became so prominent and widespread that, in 2016, the Anti-Defamation League added Pepe the Frog to its list of hate symbols.

Pepe's creator spoke out about his mortification regarding how his creation had been resignified (Furie, 2016). Despite the fact that the Pepe meme had long been used in a variety of apolitical and positive ways, and that Furie actively opposed Pepe being used by white supremacists, the image's repeated use in racist memes became a part of its connotations. Users had resignified

Pepe as a symbol of white supremacy, even though the original creator had repeatedly and publicly stated that was not the intended meaning of the cartoon. In 2017, the fast-food chain Wendy's tweeted an image of Pepe with red hair resembling the Wendy's logo. Wendy's removed the image within minutes, later stating that they had been unaware of its recent associations (Reinstein, 2017). Furie started a public campaign to "Save Pepe" in an effort to resignify the frog again in ways that rejected its association with white supremacists. After months of trying to reclaim the meaning of his own creation, Furie conceded defeat. In May 2017, he published a final Pepe comic in which he killed off the character.

Nevertheless, as we have seen, the creator of a text or image does not have absolute control over its meaning or use. Despite Furie's attempt to kill Pepe, users simply created images of him coming back to life and then resumed using him as they had before. Pepe has continued to be a frequently circulated image among white supremacist organizations. Users have also begun combining Pepe with other famous images (such as Homer Simpson or paintings by Salvador Dali) known as *Rare Pepes*. These images have been purchased at live art auctions by community members wanting to own a piece of Pepe for the equivalent of $38,500 for a single *Rare Pepe* (Klein, 2018).

Beyond highlighting the limitations of the creator in deciding what an image means, the battle over Pepe reveals how images can play a role in communicating communal identity. Because symbolic signs take on their meaning within the conventions of a particular language or culture, the same sign can have different meanings in different cultures. For most users, the "feels good man" Pepe meme carried about as much political significance as a thumbs-up emoji. But to particular communities on the 4chan and Reddit websites, Pepe represented a symbol that had gone viral in their community before becoming mainstream. Thus, the resignification of Pepe as a white supremacist symbol not only served as a way to communicate their ideology, but also as a way to reclaim communal control over who would use the image. As the Wendy's incident demonstrates, the Pepe meme developed a strong enough association with white supremacists that using it—even in ways that are not intentionally related to its resignified meaning—risks public criticism. Simply displaying the image may be perceived as a sign of support for such ideologies. Simultaneously, the image of Pepe became a popular social media profile picture among white nationalist groups and some members of the collection of political groups known as the Alt-Right. Profile images of Pepe became a way of subtly communicating a political ideology to community members who recognized the meaning, while they simply looked like a cartoon frog to those who did not. Although the image has strong associations with white supremacist communities, nothing is inherently racist about the image of the cartoon frog. If accused of using the image to communicate white supremacist beliefs, a user can simply deny knowledge of the symbol's connotations. This makes it a particularly useful symbol for communicating membership in a community.

CHECKLIST: UNDERSTANDING VISUAL CULTURE

Find an example of an image with text, an altered image, or a meme, and answer the following questions:

✓ How are viewers able to interpret the meaning of a visual sign? Is it iconic, indexical, or symbolic?

✓ What connotations are likely to be most commonly attached to this image?

✓ How does the text accompanying this image change how I interpret it?

✓ What is the dominant reading of this image? How might an oppositional reader interpret it?

✓ Am I accepting the dominant codes of this image? Do I want to?

✓ How has the meaning of this image changed over time?

✓ How have users altered this image or used it in new ways?

ANALYZING VISUAL CULTURE

National Archives at College Park[535413]

You have likely seen this poster before. What do you think the poster communicates? Since its creation by artist J. Howard Miller during World War II, the image has become a frequently displayed feminist symbol. Yet the connotations and uses associated with the image have changed dramatically over time. Over the past 75 years, the image has been largely resignified.

The woman depicted in the We Can Do It! poster spoke to the cultural anxiety of the time: As massive numbers of women were recruited to perform industrial labor, many feared the labor would render them less feminine. Miller's image thus operates within traditionally dominant codes of femininity: Notice that the woman in the image—though strong—is depicted as thin and conventionally attractive. You may be familiar with the woman in the poster as "Rosie the Riveter." Did you know the name Rosie the Riveter originally came from a painting by American artist Norman Rockwell? Rockwell's Rosie was bigger and more muscular, she had dirt on her arms and face, and she was pictured eating a sandwich; Rockwell offered an image of women doing industrial work that was far less feminine in appearance. Yet if you search for images of Rosie the Riveter, most of what you will find is the We Can Do It! poster. This is unsurprising, as the We Can Do It! image more closely matched dominant visual codes of femininity.

The image has been largely resignified through its repeated use as a visual symbol of empowerment. It no longer connotes anxiety around women in the workforce; now it tends to connote the capacity of women to roll up their sleeves and get things done. Although it began as a propaganda poster to encourage women to work harder in Westinghouse Corporation factories manufacturing war materials for the U.S. government, it is now commonly used in social movements including protests against corporate or governmental policies. At the 2017 Women's March protests in Washington, D.C., and other cities, women came dressed in navy blue with red and white bandanas. Several websites are dedicated to explaining how to dress up like the woman in the poster, and the image has even become a consistently popular Halloween costume.

6 Conclusion

Visual communication plays a bigger role in how we interact with one another than ever before. Technological advances have made visual communication more ubiquitous, and visual literacy more important, than at any time in history. In this book, we learned about visual context, the fundamental building blocks that comprise visual communication, the power of visual technologies, the role of visual rhetoric and persuasion in democracy, and how visual communication gains meaning through a variety of cultural practices. Each of these provides an important set of insights into visual communication. This chapter takes one or two ideas from each chapter and applies them to a piece of visual communication. Of course, different examples of visual communication might be better understood using different ideas from the chapters. But the goal remains the same: You should be able to examine different aspects of an image in order to develop a deeper and more complete understanding of the visual communication you encounter every day.

You may have seen this poster or images of women in hats like this on social media. You might have had some sort of positive or negative initial reaction, or you might have scrolled past them without paying much attention. But being a critical consumer of images requires you to move beyond your initial reactions, ask questions, and make connections.

In Chapter 1, we learned that visual communication never occurs in isolation, and that we should always ask what broader visual and cultural contexts an image connects to. In this case, the pink hats became prominent prior to the 2017 Women's Marches in Washington, D.C., and throughout the United States and world. The marches, in turn, originated partially as a response to Donald Trump's election as the 45th President of the United States. This particular poster extends upon that earlier context by calling supporters to the 2018 march. Even the name of the hats, dubbed by their creators as "pussyhats," has a variety of intertextual connections. Most obviously, the name is similar to the word *pussycat*, which the hats are intended to resemble. Additionally, the creators chose the name "in part as a protest against vulgar comments Donald Trump made about the freedom he felt to grab women's genitals" (*Our story*, n.d.). Choosing hats as a form of visual communication also connects to Trump's election, as his rallies were frequently attended by supporters wearing red "Make America Great Again" hats. Even the means of creating the hats connects to a long history of knitting as a traditionally feminine activity.

In Chapter 2, we learned how specific visual building blocks construct what we see. Lines combine to create shapes, visual patterns that we recognize. The design of the hats, with the protruding triangles on each corner, gives them their

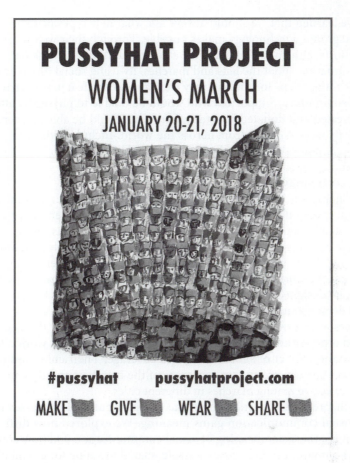

easily recognizable cat shape. In the poster, that shape is actually created by a number of smaller dots and lines that create individual shapes that you can also recognize as individuals wearing the hats. Color also plays important roles in how you see the hats and the poster (to see the poster in color, Google "pussyhat 2018 women's poster"). Of course, the most prominent color in both the hats and poster is pink. The founders of the project state that "pink is considered a very female color representing caring, compassion, and love" and that "wearing pink together is a powerful statement" (Suh and Zweiman, n.d.). Notice the different colors of the individuals in the poster. By using a variety of whites, browns, pinks, yellows, and reds, the poster presents a sense of the project as racially and ethnically diverse. This wide array of colors, combined with the absence of other visual details within each drawing, makes it easy to identify a face in the poster that looks a little like you.

In Chapter 3, we learned that technology has enabled new forms of interactivity as users can interact with both technology and other people in new ways. We learned that we should always ask what new types of social connections and groups a technology makes possible. Through their website and social media efforts, Suh and Zweiman were able to reach a massive, global audience with information about the hats and marches. By using social media to distribute the knitting plans for the hat, they were able to create a particularly unique form of community: Supporters who would be unable to physically attend the march created and donated hats for others who would be able to attend. Over 60,000 hats were donated from across the world. Included with the plans for the hat were notes prompting those who knitted the hats to communicate their names and contact information to the recipient so that they could continue forming community after the march.

In Chapter 4, we learned how visual rhetoric and persuasion play an important role in democratic societies, and how images often provide a common focus and starting point for discussions about what is going on in the world. We also learned about image events, staged actions designed to create visual content that can gain widespread circulation and challenge how viewers understand the world. Both the march itself and the role of the hats within the march were designed to serve as image events. The march was likely the largest political demonstration in U.S. history. Efforts to gain widespread circulation of the images were a tremendous success: The massive crowds at the Washington Mall and other cities captured news coverage throughout the world. The hats were also the subject of substantial news coverage. Their color and ubiquity made them visually prominent in images of the marches, and they provided a visual connection among marches in different cities.

In Chapter 5, we learned about the complex cultural processes through which visual communication gains meaning. We explored how difficult it is to determine the exact meaning of visual communication and how combining words with images can help create a stable, shared meaning for a symbol. There is, of course, no reason why a hat with pointy corners that generally mimic the shape of cat ears would serve as a unifying visual symbol among people participating in a protest. Because of this, Suh and Zweiman included a "Mission" page along with the knitting pattern for the hat. The page articulates the intended meaning of the hats, including the purpose behind their name, shape, and color. If you had seen the hats and were trying to better understand them, locating the text that originally accompanied them would provide you with important insights into what they meant to the communities that created them.

Consider how much more completely you understand the Pussyhat Project poster now. Rather than just seeing the hats and having only your initial reaction to them, you can see how the different aspects of visual communication function together. You are able to recognize how Suh and Zweiman utilized digital and social media to create a community uniting people who couldn't attend the march with those who could. You see how they used that community to help create a visual symbol that would simultaneously create a statement through its color as well as serving as a visual response to both Trump's earlier comments and his supporters' use of hats as a means of representing their support. You understand why Suh and Zweiman included a written description to help viewers interpret the hats as intended. You recognize how they then took advantage of both televised and online news media by manufacturing an image event that garnered widespread media coverage.

You can develop a deeper understanding of any piece of visual communication by learning to habitually ask questions of the images that surround you every day. Understanding visual context, recognizing an image's fundamental building blocks, or understanding the technological, rhetorical, or cultural elements of an image each offer a new set of insights into how a piece of visual communication functions. But it is when you combine all of these insights that you gain a more complete understanding of any piece of visual communication. In a world increasingly filled with visual communication that is skillfully designed to get you to buy a specific product, click a certain link, or support a particular candidate, it is more important than ever to think critically about the images you see. By equipping you with questions to ask about different aspects of visual communication, and encouraging you to explore how these elements work together, this book is intended to help you take a more active and informed role in how you see the world around you.

GLOSSARY

apparent motion the illusion of motion perceived when multiple still images are displayed in rapid succession

color the hue, value, and saturation of light reflecting off of an object or image

composition how the visual elements of an image are situated within a frame

connotative meaning the variety of meanings, attitudes, and emotions that viewers associate with a word or sign

cultivation theory the theory that television viewers gradually begin to perceive what they see on television as an accurate representation of the world

daguerreotype a photographic technique that allowed images to be developed in about ten minutes, making individual and family portraits affordable and accessible for the first time

denotative meaning the widely agreed-upon meaning that a word or sign holds within a particular community

depth how close or far away an object is, particularly in relation to other objects

dot a small, round point in space; the most basic building block of visual communication

filtering active and passive processes by which we select what we do and do not see on the Internet

frame magnetism the visual illusion that the nearer an object is to the edge of a frame, the stronger it seems that the object is being pulled toward that edge

Gestalt the perception of a whole that cannot be described simply by describing the elements that make up its parts

hue the particular color that forms when light reflects off of objects

iconic image memorable and easily-recognized image that represents significant events, stimulates emotional identification in viewers, and appears in a wide range of media

iconic sign a sign that resembles the object it represents (known as the *referent*) by depicting some recognizable quality of the referent

ideological fragmentation the consequence of individuals finding political information from sources that support their own political beliefs, while avoiding alternative perspectives

image event a staged action designed to create visual content that gains widespread circulation and attention and challenges how viewers understand the world

implied motion the illusion of movement within a single image, such as a photograph or comic book illustration

indexical signs a sign that draws upon some physical or existential relationship between the sign and the referent

interactivity how new media technologies enable users to interact with both technology and other users

intertextuality the idea that every text and image draws on and connects to past texts and images

line a series of dots placed together without any space between them

monuments visual representations of the past that provide viewers with important cues about their identity and select which people and events are worthy of remembrance and emulation

motion the illusion of movement in an image or a series of images

perceiving the mental process of making meaning out of visual stimuli

printing press Johannes Gutenberg's invention that reproduced pages more quickly and economically than ever before, allowing words and images to circulate at previously unimaginable speeds

propaganda the use of art to create an emotional response in audience members and lead them to particular political identifications, often by presenting simplified, misleading, or even false information

resignification the process by which the cultural connotation or use of a symbol is altered

Rule of Thirds the photographic principle that suggests that breaking an image into thirds, both vertically and horizontally, and placing visually important parts of the image at the intersection of these thirds will yield more interesting images

saturation the purity and intensity of a color, occurring on a continuum from the specific hue to gray

selecting choosing particular visual stimuli to focus on

semiotics the study of how signs take on and communicate meaning

sensing the physiological act of seeing as a result of light bouncing off of objects and into the eye

shape a visual pattern that we recognize

symbolic signs signs whose meaning depends on learned social conventions

value the darkness or lightness of a particular hue

visual communication the use of visual symbols to create and share meaning or to encourage action

visual culture culture in which viewing ubiquitous visual media is central to how individuals and groups understand themselves and the world; can also refer to the academic study of such cultures

visual literacy the ability to skillfully interpret and evaluate visual communication

REFERENCES

Chapter 1

Bamford, A. (2003). *The visual literacy white paper.* [White paper]. Retrieved January 24, 2016, from https://www.aperture.org/wp-content/uploads/2013/05/visual-literacy-wp.pdf

Barthes, R. (1977). The death of the author. In S. Heath (Ed. & Trans.) *Image music text* (pp. 142–146). London: Fontana.

Bedford, S. (2002). *Aldous Huxley: A biography.* Chicago: Ivan R. Dee.

Huxley, A. (1942). *The art of seeing.* NY: Harper and Brothers.

Lester, P. M. (2014). *Visual communication: Images with messages* (6th Ed.). Boston, MA: Cengage.

Tyley, J. (2015, September 23). The science of vision: How do our eyes see? *The Independent.* Retrieved from http://www.independent.co.uk/life-style/health-and-families/features/the-science-of-vision-how-do-our-eyes-see-10513902.html

Chapter 2

Anderson, J. & Anderson, B. (1993). The myth of persistence of vision revisited. *Journal of Film and Video, 45*(1), 3–12.

Arntson, A. E. (2012). *Graphic design basics* (6th Ed.). Boston, MA: Wadsworth, Cengage Learning.

Dondis, D. A. (1973). *A primer on visual literacy.* Cambridge, MA: The Massachusetts Institute of Technology Press.

Elliot, A. J., & Niesta, D. (2008). Romantic red: Red enhances men's attraction to women. *Journal of Personality and Social Psychology, 95*, 1150–1164. doi: 10.1037/0022-3514.95.5.1150

Fabos, B. (2013). Visual Literacy: Aesthetics, Semiotics, and the Truth Behind an Image. In J. Jensen, D. Gomery, R. Campbell, B. Fabos, & J. Frechette (Eds.), *Media in Society* (pp. 52–77). New York: Bedford/St. Martin.

Guéguen, N., & Jacob, C. (2013). Color and cyber-attractiveness: Red enhances men's attraction to women's internet personal ads. *Color Research & Application, 38*, 309–312. doi:10.1002/col.21718

Kanizsa, G. (1979). *Organization in vision: Essays on Gestalt perception.* NY: Preager.

Loreto, V., Mukherjee, A., & Tria, F. (2012). On the origin of the hierarchy of color names. *Proceedings of the National Academy of Sciences of the United States of America, 109*(18), 6819–6824. doi:10.1073/pnas.1113347109

Newbold, C. (2013). Red and yellow make us eat: How restaurants suck us in. *The VCG.* Retrieved from http://thevisualcommunicationguy.com/2013/10/13/red-and-yellow-how-restaurants-suck-us-in

Wertheimer, M. (1938). Laws in organizational and perceptual form. In W. Ellis (Ed. & Trans.) *A sourcebook of Gestalt psychology.* (pp. 71–88). London: Routledge & Kegan Paul. (Original work published 1923).

Wong, B. (2010). Points of view: Gestalt principles (Part 1). *Nature Methods, 7*(11), 863–864. doi: 10.1038/nmeth1110-863.

Chapter 3

Deluca, K. M., & Demo, A. T. (2000). Imagining nature: Watkins, Yosemite, and the birth of environmentalism. *Critical Studies in Media Communication, 17*(3), 241–260.

Dirks, T. (n.d.). *The history of film.* Retrieved from http://www.filmsite.org/pre20sintro.html

Febvre, L., & Martin, H. (1976). *The coming of the book: The impact of printing, 1450–1800* (D. Gerard, Trans.). London: Verso.

Finnegan, C. A. (2001). The naturalistic enthymeme and visual argument: Photographic representation in the "skull controversy." *Argumentation and Advocacy, 37*(3), 133–149.

Folkenflik, D. (2013). *Murdoch's world: The last of the old media empires.* NY: PublicAffairs.

Gerbner, G. & Gross, L. (1976). Living with television: The violence profile. *Journal of Communication, 26*(2), 172–194.

Hughes, M. (1980). The fruits of cultivation analysis: A reexamination of some effects of television watching. *Public Opinion Quarterly, 44*(3), 287–302.

Innis, H. A. (1951). *The bias of communication.* Toronto, University of Toronto Press.

Leiner, B. M., Cerf, V. G., Clark, D. D., Kahn, R. E., Kleinrock, L., Lynch, D. C., Postel, J., Roberts, L.G., & Wolff, S. (2009). A brief history of the internet. *Computer Communication Review, 39*(5), 22–31.

Miller, K. (2016, December 5). Confessions of an anonymous Victoria's Secret photoshopper. *Refinery29.* Retrieved from http://www.refinery29.com/2016/07/117242/victoria-secret-photoshopping-tricks-interview

The partisan divide on political values grows even wider. (2017, October 5). Pew Research Center. Retrieved from http://www.people-press.org/2017/10/05/the-partisan-divide-on-political-values-grows-even-wider

Pfister, D. S., & Woods, C. S. (2016). The unnaturalistic enthymeme: Figuration, interpretation, and critique after digital mediation. *Argumentation and Advocacy, 52*, 236–253.

Sandvine. (2015). *Global internet phenomena: Latin America and North America* [White paper]. Retrieved December 13, 2017, from https://www.sandvine.com/hubfs/downloads/archive/2015-global-internet-phenomena-report-latin-america-and-north-america.pdf

Schooler, D., Ward, L. M., Merriwether, A., & Carruthers, A. (2004). Who's that girl: Television's role in the body image development of young white and black women. *Psychology of Women Quarterly, 28*(1), 38–47. doi: 10.1111/j.1471-6402.2004.00121.x

Sturken, M., & Cartwright, L. (2009). *Practices of looking: An introduction to visual culture.* NY: Oxford University Press.

Sunstein, C. (2007). *Republic.com 2.0.* Princeton, NJ: Princeton University Press.

Chapter 4

Blair, C., Dickinson, G., & Ott, B. L. (2010). *Places of public memory: The rhetoric of museums and memorials.* Tuscaloosa, AL: University of Alabama Press.

Capra, F. (1971). *The name above the title: An autobiography.* New York: Macmillan.

Dauber, C. (2014). The branding of violent Jihadism. In C. Winkler and C. Dauber (Eds.) *Visual extremism and propaganda in the online environment* (pp. 137–163). Carlisle, PA: United States Army War College Press.

Delicath, J. W., & Deluca, K. M. (2003). Image events, the public sphere, and argumentative practice: The case of radical environmental groups. *Argumentation, 17*(3), 315–333.

Deluca, K. (1999). *Image politics: The new rhetoric of environmental activism.* New York, NY: Routledge.

Fish, L. (1987). *The last firebase: A guide to the Vietnam Veterans Memorial.* Shippensburg, PA: White Mane.

Forgery, B. (1991, September 20). Battle won for war memorials: CFA approves women's Vietnam, black patriot designs. *Washington Post*, 18.

Hariman, R., & Lucaites, J. L. (2007). *No caption needed: Iconic photographs, public culture, and liberal democracy.* Chicago, IL: The University of Chicago Press.

Lester, P. M. (2014). *Visual communication: Images with messages* (6th Ed.). Boston, MA: Cengage.

Manes, C. (1990). *Green rage: Radical environmentalism, and the unmaking of civilization.* Boston: Little, Brown.

McGeough, R. E. (2011). *The American counter-monumental tradition: Renegotiating public memory and the evolution of American sacred space* (Doctoral dissertation). Retrieved from https://digitalcommons.lsu.edu/gradschool_dissertations/2556

Olson, L. C., Finnegan, C. A., & Hope, D. S. (Eds.) (2008). *Visual rhetoric: A reader in communication and American culture.* Thousand Oaks, CA: SAGE Publications.

Perry, S. P. & Long, J. M. (2015). Visual recoveries of the holy war. Paper presented at the 2015 *NCA/AFA Summer Conference on Argumentation,* Alta, UT.

Riefenstahl, L. (1935). *The triumph of the will* [motion picture]. Germany.

Rosenzweig, R., & Thelen, D. (1998). *The presence of the past.* New York, NY: Columbia University Press.

Scruggs, J. C., & Swerdlow, J. L. (1985). *To heal a nation: The Vietnam Veterans Memorial.* New York, NY: Harper Collins.

Sturken, M. (1997). *Tangled memories: The Vietnam war, the AIDS epidemic, and the politics of remembering.* Berkeley, CA: University of California Press.

Watson, P. (2005, May 10). One day on the water with Bob Hunter. *Sea Shepherd Conservation Society.* Retrieved from http://www.seashepherd.fr/news-and-media/editorial-050510-1.html

Chapter 5

Atkin, A. (2013). Peirce's Theory of Signs, *The Stanford Encyclopedia of Philosophy* (Summer 2013 Edition), Edward N. Zalta (Ed.). Retrieved from https://plato.stanford.edu/archives/sum2013/entries/peirce-semiotics

Barthes, R. (1977). *Elements of semiology* (A. Lavers and C. Smith, Trans.). NY: Hill and Wang. (Original work published 1964).

Butler, J. (1993). *Bodies that matter: On the discursive limits of sex.* NY: Routledge.

Chandler, D. (1994): *Semiotics for beginners.* Retrieved from http://visual-memory.co.uk/daniel/Documents/S4B/sem01.html

Dawkins, R. (1976). *The selfish gene.* Oxford, UK: Oxford University.

Furie (2016, October 13). Pepe the Frog's creator: I'm reclaiming him. He was never about hate. *Time.* Retrieved from http://time.com/4530128/pepe-the-frog-creator-hate-symbol

Hall, S. (1993). Encoding, decoding. In S. During (Ed.), *The cultural series reader* (pp. 507–517). New York, NY: Routledge.

Kennerly, M., & Pfister, D. S. (Eds.). (2018). *Ancient rhetorics + digital networks.* Tuscaloosa, AL: University of Alabama Press.

Klein, J. (2018, January 19). *I went to the first live auction for Rare Pepes on the blockchain. Motherboard.* Retrieved from https://motherboard.vice.com/en_us/article/ev57p4/i-went-to-the-first-live-auction-for-rare-pepes-on-the-blockchain

Mahler, J. (2015, February 27). The white and gold (no, blue and black!) dress that melted the Internet. *New York Times.* Retrieved from https://www.nytimes.com/2015/02/28/business/a-simple-question-about-a-dress-and-the-world-weighs-in.html

McGeough, R. E. & McGeough, D. D. (2014). Starving to live: Self-mutilation as public argument in the Columbian hunger strikes. In C. H. Palczewski (Ed.). *Disturbing argument* (pp. 99–104). New York: Routledge.

Palczewski, C. H., Ice, R., & Fritch, J. (2016). *Rhetoric and civic life* (2nd Ed.). State Park, PA: Strata.

Reinstein (2017, January 4). Wendy's tweeted (and quickly deleted) a Pepe meme. *BuzzFeed News.* Retrieved from https://www.buzzfeed.com/juliareinstein/wendys-pepe?utm_term=.gaqxGEXakq#.bvZjLdKX3Z

Chapter 6

Our story. (n.d.). Retrieved from https://www.pussyhatproject.com/our-story

Suh, K., & Zweiman, J. (n.d.). *Pussyhat Project pattern and manifesto.* Retrieved from https://drive.google.com/file/d/0BwBjtQGbV7gEZU1TdUd2b1JIZGM/view018-flyer.pdf

INDEX